27

Over Here!

Also by Lorraine Diehl

★ ★

The Late, Great Pennsylvania Station

The Automat:
The History, Recipes, and Allure of Horn
and Hardart's Masterpiece

Subways:
The Tracks That Built New York City

HERE!

New York City During World War II

LORRAINE B. DIEHL

 Smithsonian Books

An Imprint of HarperCollinsPublishers
www.harpercollins.com

HarperCollins books may be purchased for educational, business, or sales promotional use. For information, please write: Special Markets Department, HarperCollins Publishers, 10 East 53rd Street, New York, NY 10022.

An extension of this copyright page appears on page 255.

FIRST EDITION

Designed by Suet Yee Chong

Library of Congress Cataloging-in-Publication Data
Diehl, Lorraine B.
    Over here!: New York city during World War II / Lorraine B. Diehl.
        p. cm.
    Includes bibliographic references and index.
    ISBN: 978-0-06-143134-0 (alk. paper)
    1. New York (N.Y.)—History—1898–1951. 2. World War, 1939–1945—New York (State)—New York. I. Title.
        F128.5.D54 2010
        940.53'7471-dc22

                                                            2009027614

10 11 12 13 14   ov/qw   10 9 8 7 6 5 4 3 2 1

For Teddy and for Lyla

★ ★

Contents

★ ★

Preface

★ ★

It was a single image that drew me into the story of New York City during World War II. A newspaper account contrasting the building used for the 1945 espionage thriller *The House on 92nd Street* with the actual storefront in York-ville intrigued me. That storefront, with its disturbing displays, was what got my attention. In the early 1930s, one could stop by 309 East 92nd Street and pick up a swastika banner or two, some pamphlets heralding Adolf Hitler as the savior of the Aryan Nation, and all manner of anti-Semitic tracts. There was information on a camp on Long Island and one in New Jersey where German-American children were being indoctrinated into an American version of Hitler Youth. But then, just a crosstown bus away, one would be delivered onto the streets of the Upper West Side where newly arrived German Jews, with the startling optimism of the New York skyline still in their heads, were settling in.

Pearl Harbor changed everything and like Americans across the country, New Yorkers rose to the occasion, enlisting, volunteering, and sacrificing for the war effort. But there is much more to the story of New York City during World War II. Because England's ability to defend itself against Germany depended on fuel and supplies loaded on ships leaving New York Harbor, German U-boats came to call, so deadly at times that area beaches were closed and lights facing the ocean were extinguished. Just as the U-boat menace subsided, fear of an attack by air kept the city's skyscrapers in darkness. Manhattan Island was a very real target for Hitler, who pinpointed spots he wanted bombed. As threats from sea and air kept everyone vigilant, New Yorkers were also acting as hosts to American servicemen and women who were enjoying a few days' leave, as well as to those soldiers and sailors from Allied countries whose ships were in port. Times Square, with its nightclubs and Broadway shows and the celebrity-filled Stage Door Canteen, became the great release valve. In many New York homes, there was an extra place at the Thanksgiving table for servicemen away from home.

It was in New York City that the atomic bomb, code-named the Manhattan Project, was born. It was also here, in a modest office in Rockefeller Center, that a Canadian millionaire, working for the British Secret Service, oversaw a vast network of spies. Pier 88 at West 49th Street was where the SS *Normandie* caught fire and burned, sparking rumors of sabotage. Although that rumor proved false, four German spies did come ashore on a Long Island beach one foggy night in June of 1942, with instructions to bomb, among other targets, the Hell Gate Bridge and Newark's Pennsylvania Station.

Fortunately, New York was spared the saboteurs' deadly plans, and except for the occasional blackout, rationed food, and little gas in the tank, New Yorkers had few obstacles to keep them from doing their part for the war effort. Because New York City was not harmed by the war, most New Yorkers living through those emotional times have warm memories of a city pulling together at a very sober time. Sobriety was not a priority on V-J Day, however, when every stoop on every block became the scene of an instant party. Times Square gathered the rest of the city in celebration as its great neon signs, unrestricted by the dim-out, blazed through the night.

Nowhere was the war's end more dramatic than along the city's waterfront, where almost daily, welcoming crowds lined up to watch the great ocean liners filled with returning troops steam through the Narrows into the city's famous harbor. Jack Wayman, who arrived on the *Queen Mary*, remembers it well: "To come up that river and see the Statue of Liberty, to dock and have crowds of people running to greet you . . . that was thrilling."

The end of the war changed the city. It loosened the umbilical cord that tied neighborhoods to "the old country," making way for the new "international city" as defined by the complex of buildings rising on the East River. The United Nations would set the tone. Sleek glass boxes began to rise along Manhattan's commercial avenues, catching the face of the sun as they loomed over older brick "wedding cake" buildings. "Pre-war" was a new term, defining that Mason-Dixon line in architecture. As for those old neighborhoods, many would change or disappear as returning veterans with the ink hardly dry on their GI loans left the city for the new suburbs. The storefront on 92nd Street was still there, but the days when it sold the paraphernalia of the death machine that took out six million were now a dark footnote to the city's past. Most New Yorkers needed to tuck that history away for a while and look toward the future. A new decade was just four short years away after all, and New Yorkers were anxious to embrace it.

World War II ended sixty-five years ago and yet its lessons still resonate. Once again we are asked to ration our resources, not to fuel a world war but to keep our exhausted planet from depletion. Sacrifice is a noble notion again as we look out over the debris field of our past indulgences. The cost of those indulgences—to our souls as well as the planet that sustains us—has been high, and it should humble us all to realize how small our sacrifice is when placed against a generation that was called upon to give up so much more than gas for their cars and choice cuts of meat for their tables. The Americans who emerged from World War II cherished the fruits of their shared sacrifice because always in their minds there was an image of the terrible world they might have inherited. We already have that hindsight. All we need do is follow their example.

PART I

SHADOWS OVER MANHATTAN

New York City on the Eve of War

THE AMERICAN VERSION of Hitler Youth enjoying their moment in the sun at Camp Siegfried. The 44-acre "Little Germany" in Yaphank, Long Island was blatantly spawning a mini-Aryan nation.

Nazis Among Us

"In a year, perhaps less than a year, they will all be taking orders from us."

Conrad Veidt as Franz Ebbing
All Through the Night
Warner Bros., 1942

The scene was the cellar of a seedy saloon on Second Avenue in the Yorkville section of Manhattan. The time, late evening in early February 1934. Sometime in January, a tenant in the building where the saloon operated dropped a line to Representative Samuel Dickstein's office in Washington, D.C., informing him that he had seen uniformed men with swastikas on their armbands enter the saloon and then disappear. Richard Rollins, who was working unofficially for Dickstein's subcommittee investigating Nazi propaganda in this country, contacted the building's landlord asking to be informed the next time these men appeared. Now, the phone call Rollins had been waiting for came through. Within minutes, Rollins joined the landlord and together they descended the steps into the cellar. The first thing Rollins noticed was a cement wall separating the boiler room from a second, smaller room. Placing his hands over the wall, Rollins discovered that the mortar sealing the cement blocks was slightly damp. He got down on his knees and began scooping some of it out, eventually managing to pull away a few of the concrete blocks. Then he waited.

At 10:00 P.M. the sound of boot steps could be heard, and then an overhead light bulb was turned on in the room. Rollins described what he saw in the glaring light:

> The room, about fifteen feet by twenty, was a detailed reproduction of a Berlin Storm Troop cellar . . . I counted twenty-two uniformed men. Brown shirts, breeches, boots, Sam Browne belts with pistol holsters. Their Troop Fuehrer faced them. He lifted his arm half-way, elbow close to his side, palm out and clipped "Heil Hitler!"

Rollins, who would write a book about his experience, went on to record the Troop Fuehrer's words as he pointed to an American flag on which was sewn a huge swastika: *"This is the flag we shall carry through the streets of New York when we wipe them clean of the Jewish scum."* The men were then instructed to show up at the Hudson River pier the next afternoon where the *Albert Balin,* a German liner, would dock. Once onboard, they would discard the trousers they wore under winter coats and put on two Nazi uniforms, repeating this maneuver later that evening until each of them had brought four Nazi uniforms into the city.

The scene plays like one from *All Through the Night,* in which Humphrey Bogart stumbles upon a group of Nazis operating out of the basement of an Upper East Side auction house and poses as one of them during a meeting. The film had comic undertones and in some ways, so did this attempt to turn New York City and eventually the entire country into an extension of the Fatherland.

In the 1930s, Yorkville—an area on the east side of Manhattan stretching from 57th to 96th Street—was a working-class neighborhood, home to Hungarians, Poles, Germans, Czechs, Slovaks, and Irish, with a small community of Italians at its northern border. But to anyone walking across 86th Street from Lexington Avenue to the East River, this was Germantown, and 86th Street was affectionately known as Sauerkraut Boulevard. Here one could take in *Das Blaue von Him-*

mel, the new German film at the Casino Theatre, and pick up a copy of the German-American newspaper the *New Yorker Staats-Zeitung* at a corner newsstand before dropping into the Kleine Konditerei or Café Geiger for a *kaffee mit schlag* and a slice of Sacher torte. The Brauhaus and Café Hindenburg served up sauerbraten and wiener schnitzel with bottles of *liebfraumilch* to wash them down. On the north side of the street, Ger-

man couples danced to the Lorelei's polka band, followed by a thirst-quenching tankard of Spaten or Dinkel Acker served up at the dance hall's famous horseshoe bar.

By the time Rollins was spying on those brown-shirts in the saloon basement, a thirty-nine-year-old former photoengraver from Magdeburg was holding his own meetings in the Turnhalle, just above the Jaegerhaus, a popular restaurant on the corner of 85th Street and Lexington Avenue. Heinz Spanknoebel was about to be named leader of The Friends of the New Germany by the American arm of Hitler's Nazi Party, and while patrons below were dining on rabbit and venison, Spanknoebel, sporting a thick cropped mustache, was whipping twelve hundred men into a patriotic frenzy until

THIS YORKVILLE STOREFRONT at 309 East 92nd Street served as headquarters for Paul Manger's Gau-USA, a precursor to the American Bund. Meetings were held in a back room. Nazi paraphernalia can be seen in the window.

SHOT IN SEMI-documentary style, the plot for *The House on 92nd Street* tapped into the story of William Sebold, a German-born double agent working for the FBI. The film's exterior shots substituted the original storefront for an elegant townhouse on 93rd Street off Park Avenue.

they all rose and shouted *"Heil Hitler"* for the whole neighborhood to hear.

Yorkville, like the rest of the city, was suffering through the Depression. On any given winter night in 1931, Jacob Ruppert and George Ehret could look out their drawing-room windows at Central Park and catch the glow from the fires lit by the destitute who were living in the Hoover Valley shanties just behind the Metropolitan Museum of Art. The two beer-makers and their giant breweries employed many of the men who lived in this neighborhood. The enterprising Ruppert, who would buy the New York Yankees and build Yankee Stadium, was known to install bars on the ground floors of tenements with the caveat that they be stocked exclusively with his Knickerbocker beer. It may well have been in one of Ruppert's bars where the Nazi meeting Richard Rollins spied on that February night was held.

For the people who lived in those tenements—the cigar-makers, shopkeepers, and factory workers—life was now barely hand-to-mouth. It was these people, the first- and second-generation German-Americans in New York City and throughout the country, locked in economic despair, whom Heinz Spanknoebel—himself a victim of the Depression when he was dismissed from the Detroit Ford Motor plant—wanted to win over.

Spanknoebel wasn't the first Nazi to try to leave his boot prints all over Yorkville. Another German national, this one an out-of-work janitor, headed the first Nazi Party here. Paul Manger and his Gau-USA had taken over a storefront at 309 East 92nd Street, an address that would be used for the 20th Century-Fox 1945 spy movie *The House on 92nd Street.*

From there, his 1,500-member mini Aryan Nation handed out pamphlets portraying Hitler as the savior of Germany and the Jews as the cause of all the bad things that were happening to them. Manger had just held a meeting in Kreuzer Hall on East 86th Street, rousing 250 German nationals to call for the ouster of all Jews from Germany, when orders came from Berlin to stop. It was 1933. Hitler was now securely in power and Franklin Roosevelt, America's new president, was casting a suspicious eye on Germany's National Socialism. Now was not the time to give Roosevelt any cause for concern.

If Rudolf Hess, Hitler's Deputy Fuehrer, was looking for a more subtle spokesman for the Nazi cause, he didn't choose well. With his dark-brown hair parted to one side and his mustache trimmed in the fashion of the Fuehrer, Spanknoebel was a startling figure. At one point he marched into the offices of the prestigious *New Yorker Staats-Zeitung und Herald* at 22 William Street, the largest German-language newspaper in America. Flashing a document signed by Rudolf Hess that officially recognized him as the leader of The Friends of the New Germany, he ordered Bernard and Victor Ridder, the publishers, to stop publishing Jewish propaganda and print articles favorable to Hitler and Nazi Germany. (Just four months before, their newspaper had printed an editorial condemning Hitler and his persecution of the Jews.) An astounded Victor Ridder threw Spanknoebel out of his office and called the police.

The fact of the matter was that most German-Americans were either embarrassed by these brown-shirts or viewed them as curiosities. Even though the Nazis had pushed themselves into middle America—to Chicago and Detroit and across the Hudson, where a lively lot of them were making mischief in Union City, New Jersey—their appeal was mainly with the recent immigrants, many of whom were disenfranchised German nationals whose allegiance remained with the Fatherland.

Spanknoebel was obviously living his own fantasy. The day after an anti-Nazi parade took place in Yorkville and simultaneously in parts of Brooklyn, the new Aryan leader invited his fellow Nazis for an evening cruise around Manhattan Island on the German steamer SS *Resolute*. Decked out in full uniform, they hoisted their steins and belted out *"Deutschland, Deutschland über Alles"* with the New York skyline and Statue of Liberty serving as backdrop. This inebriated group had convinced themselves that they were on their way to establishing a true Nazi party in America.

Eight days later, Spanknoebel was back in the Turnhalle, this time insisting that the Nazi flag be flown at New York City's German Day Parade. The October 29th celebration was going to commemorate the 250th anniversary of the arrival of the first German settlers to America. When Spanknoebel was turned down he flew into a rage, dispatching his troops throughout the city to paint swastikas on the doors of Jewish synagogues. As a result of his antics, German Day was officially canceled in New York City and a warrant for his arrest was issued by the United States Justice Department on the grounds that he was

THE NAZI FLAG FLIES HIGH AS GERMAN-AMERICAN BUNDISTS joined the German Day Parade making its way across East 86th Street. The date was October 30, 1939, one month after Britain and France declared war on Germany.

an unregistered foreign agent. It was time to get the troublesome leader out of the picture. Fearing that Spanknoebel would rather take his chances with the American justice system than face the music back in Berlin, Joseph Goebbels, Hitler's new propaganda chief, ordered Spanknoebel brought back to Germany. On October 27, Spanknoebel was kidnapped while dining at the home of Dr. Ignatz Griebl, a respected New York surgeon and obstetrician who also happened to be a Nazi, and two days later he was put on the SS *Europa* bound for Bremen.

With the brown-shirts flexing their muscles all over Yorkville, New Yorkers began looking at every German-American with suspicion. In a number of cases, those suspicions were well founded. Subway patrolman Larry Karlin, who happened to be Jewish, went into a change booth at a station in heavily German Ridgewood, Queens, when the clerk muttered in German: "Isn't it wonderful? When Hitler comes to power here he's going to put all of the Jews in a concentration camp." Yetta Guy, who worked in a courthouse during the 1930s, remembers a friend's reception when he went into Yorkville: "He was on his way to a lecture and he was beaten up." Clifford Foster, former staff counsel to the American Civil Liberties Union, says, "If you went into a tavern in Yorkville and weren't pro-Hitler, you'd be given a hard

time." That bartender at the Lorelei, the waiter at Café Geiger, the counterman at Karl Ehmer's slicing your liverwurst—any of them could be a Nazi spy.

Then, in the early morning hours of February 6, 1934, New Yorkers' suspicions were confirmed. For months U.S. customs and federal agents had been watching Pier 42, which stretched along the Hudson River waterfront from 45th to 46th Street. This was where the North German Lloyd Line's steamships berthed. The agents would regularly board German liners with their swastikas hung in ballrooms and portraits of Hitler on every available wall, looking for the Nazi propaganda that was finding its way into the country. It was a known fact that many of the ships' crews were Nazi agents and that transatlantic couriers were feeding the Nazi espionage machine. On that Tuesday morning, U.S. agents boarded the *Este*, a German freighter that had just docked. This time their search paid off. In a cook's locker they found six burlap sacks containing three hundred pounds of pamphlets and booklets—some of which contained Hitler's recent speeches—all printed in German. The packets inside the sacks were to go to agents in Detroit, Cincinnati, and Chicago, and in New York to an address in Yorkville—152 East 83rd Street—where Spanknoebel had set up The Friends of the New Germany.

The heat was on when in March, Congressman Samuel Dickstein from New York, a man whose parents had escaped the pogroms, vowed to "eradicate all traces of Nazism in the United States." During that same month, twenty thousand New Yorkers showed up at Madison Square Garden to witness a mock trial against Hitler, sponsored by the American Jewish Congress. The vise was about to get even tighter. In September 1933, Rabbi Stephen S. Wise, New York City's outspoken anti-Nazi Zionist, persuaded the United States government to join a world boycott of products coming from Germany as a means of protesting Hitler's treatment of Jews. A few months later that boycott was tightened when it was discovered that German products were getting phony labels and slipping through.

German-American shopkeepers were furious. How could they stock the specialty items—the *apfelmus* and the wursts—their customers expected if they were prohibited from getting them? Enter The Friends of the New Germany with stickers emblazoned with blue Nazi-like eagles. These stickers were placed in the windows of the butcher shops and grocery stores that were now boycotting the boycott. The shopkeepers felt they were defending their rights to conduct business. The way most New Yorkers saw it, that label placed those who displayed it on the side

of Hitler. As for The Friends of the New Germany, they believed they were finally getting German-Americans to see themselves as Germans living in America rather than Americans of German descent.

The idea that German-Americans were denouncing the American boycott on German imports was putting a further strain on America's near-moribund relations with Germany. A month later, in February, after the hearings had been broadcast over the airwaves and printed in newspapers throughout the country, a report by Dickstein and Congressman John McCormack of Massachusetts made it official: the Nazi Party in America was turning German-Americans against their own country.

Just a few months before, on a hot July evening, a group of sailors led by seaman Bill Bailey boarded the SS *Bremen* as it was about to sail for Germany, ripped the giant swastika from the bowsprit, and tossed it into the Hudson River. The incident, which made the *New York Times*, became symbolic of the anti-Nazi sentiment that was growing stronger in New York City.

With relations between Germany and America at a new low, the order from Berlin was issued: On December 31, 1935, at the stroke of midnight, any German national still affiliated with The Friends of the New Germany risked losing his

German citizenship. It was a pretty serious threat, except no one was listening. In spite of Hitler's edict, America's Nazis believed there was a place for them in America.

In fact, the time was ripe for a real American Fuehrer, a guy who could once and for all stomp his boot on a New York City sidewalk and let the truth sink in: America wanted and needed National Socialism. In spite of the nasty things President "Rosenfeld" was saying about fascism, Hitler believed that it was the only way to get everyone on the same page. So did another man.

If Fritz Julius Kuhn wasn't born, Mel Brooks would have invented him. The Munich-born former chemist came on the scene when The Friends of the New Germany was on the ropes after getting orders from Berlin to close up shop. Giving themselves a new name, the Amerikadeutscher Volksbund—a.k.a. the Bund—they hastily swore Kuhn in as their new president. They had to know what they were in for when their new leader dropped the title "president"— it was too American—and insisted on being addressed as "Bundesleiter." Kuhn had an ego as big as his plans for the new Aryan America. Writer Sander A. Diamond's description of him is a résumé begging for a role in *The Producers*:

"Like the German Fuhrer, he regarded himself as a great man, a man chosen to unify his racial brothers in America. He was rarely out of uniform. His black leather jack boots apparently glued to his six-foot frame, his thinning hair slicked back over his broad head, his legs apart, and his thumbs fixed in his Sam Browne belt, Kuhn loudly proclaimed himself the American Fuhrer."

From his heavily guarded Yorkville office at 178 East 85th Street, Kuhn went into overdrive, feeding anti-Roosevelt articles to the Bund's house organ, which was distributed all over New York City; delivering speeches from the stage of the Yorkville Casino, the neighborhood's meeting and dance hall; and rallying with Father Coughlin, the anti-Semitic Catholic priest who stood firmly on the side of fascism. Strutting about in his Nazi uniform, Kuhn's presence in Yorkville was very contentious. "Across the street from his Deutsch Bund headquarters was a union hall and they would raid each others meetings," says Yorkville native Kathy Jolowicz.

Kuhn was everywhere, preaching the Aryan dream. He was in Ridgewood, Queens; at the Schwabenhalle between Knickerbocker and Myrtle avenues in Brooklyn; and at Ebling's Casino on St. Ann's Avenue in the Bronx, where the Bund held regular Thursday "Beer Eve-

nings." He gave speeches, held parades, and even organized a few torchlight rallies. Bill Vericker, who was fourteen years old when he moved into Yorkville with his German-born mother, saw Kuhn at a street rally on 86th Street: "Unless you were extremely pro-German you'd think, 'This guy is a lot of baloney.'"

Kuhn was an excellent businessman who very quickly had a cottage industry of Nazi paraphernalia humming. No longer would German uniforms have to be sneaked off German ships; the Bund had their own tailor in Queens whipping them up. A German import house in the West Forties supplied him with signet rings and emblems. And the Bund's very own printing presses kept spewing out its propaganda not far from Kuhn's Yorkville office.

In the evenings, when he wasn't stirring up his Nazi brew, Fritz was seen on the town, at jazz clubs digging the beat of that decadent "Negroid" music, or at Leon & Eddie's, the Crillon Bar, or the Swing Club, tapping his boots to a favorite, "Flat Foot Floogee with the Floy Floy." Leaving the little *frau* and the two *kinder* at home, Kuhn liked to indulge his appetite for good champagne and gourmet food in the company of attractive women, including a former Miss America.

For a guy who once worked the Ford assembly line in Detroit, being the American Fuehrer was a sweet thing. Never mind that he had the charisma of a phlegmatic accountant, that his American syntax was pretty bad, and his voice was flat and colorless. So what if he looked more like a white-collar pencil pusher than America's answer to the Jewish problem? Kuhn had put the American Bund on the map!

And now there was that new summer camp in Yaphank, Long Island, a forty-four-acre spread with its own lake where an American version of Hitler Youth could be trained and readied. Just four miles from Camp Upton, the World War I army training camp where Private Irving Berlin wrote "Oh, How I Hate to Get Up in the Morning" for his Broadway-bound revue *Yip Yip Yaphank!*, Camp Siegfried was an Aryan paradise. What good German could resist the pitch:

> When the weekend approaches, we are just longing to leave the pavements, the crowded thoroughfares, the dust, the noise of the city behind to find peace and health restoring recreation at some quiet retreat among people whose friendship we treasure.
>
> Camp Siegfried . . . will remind you of those beautiful summer excursion resorts in the old homeland and of the pleasant hours you used to spend there. You will not regret a weekend excursion to 'Camp Sieg-

fried.' For at the camp you will meet people that think as you do . . . cheerful people, honest and sincere, law-abiding!

Each Sunday morning at 8:00, hundreds of Bundists and their families descended on Pennsylvania Station and boarded the "Camp Siegfried Special." Some of them were in black boots, gray shirts, and Sam Browne belts as they sang the "Horst Wessel Song," the new Nazi anthem.

Gangway! Gangway! Now for the Brown battalions! they chanted as the train sped past sleepy Long Island towns. At the Yaphank station, a small army of uniformed children greeted them and together they marched through the town of Brookhaven, swastikas waving as an eighteen-piece tuba-led band played *Der Spielmannszug*. At the edge of the camp rose the Lakeside Inn, where under an oversized photo of an unsmiling Hitler, one could enjoy *rulufleclass* (potato balls) with knockwurst and sauerkraut, and perhaps some Hackerbrau or Rhine wine. A lot of *heil*ing went on at the Inn as strains from Wagner drifted through the air. Outside, even nature was forced to *heil*. On the lawn grew a giant swastika—the length of two tall men—made of bright red salvia and boxwood.

Of course, Camp Siegfried was not

about a day in the country. It was a giant, hopefully unobserved, recruiting center, a kind of twisted Outward Bound where not just Bundists, but all German-Americans would see that America's future was a Hitlerian future. By the summer of 1937, Kuhn would have twenty-four camps throughout the country, including Camp Nordland, across the Hudson River in rural Sussex County, New Jersey.

Fritz Kuhn's plans for America were not small: There would be a war—a big one—between the purebreds who lived here and "those blood-sucking Semites." The purebreds would win, of course, and if the Jews did not go quietly into that dark night, they would be eliminated.

By 1936, Kuhn felt Germany calling. It was the year of the summer Olympics, and they were being held in Berlin. On June 23, Kuhn, along with two hundred of his Bundists, boarded the SS *New York* for a ten-day journey to Hamburg. Kuhn was on a roll. Not only did he get to meet Hitler, he got his photo taken with the great man. There he was on the front page of all those American newspapers shaking hands with the new leader of the world! How could anyone not get the message

The FBI raided German homes in the middle of dinner because someone reported that a family had a shortwave radio.

—KATHY JOLOWICZ

and see that he, Fritz Kuhn, was part of that destiny?

Everyone did get the message. Not just the Bundists and Jew-haters, but ordinary Americans who were suddenly jolted out of their complacency. It was one thing to tolerate these men in their strange uniforms walking the streets of Yorkville as they preached the glories of a new Germany; it was quite another to see their leader shaking hands with the man who was poised to goose-step his way across Europe. Public opinion was swift and strong: Kuhn and his Volksbund were agents of Hitler, with a mission to bring down American democracy.

Fritz Kuhn pushed on. He was always a liar, but now the lies became grander. He was, he told his followers, a valuable player in Hitler's new world order. Hitler had told him so! He was actually a loose cannon, gathering speed and propelled by nothing more than his delusions. Bundists began jumping ship. Some of them went back to Germany. Shopkeepers in Yorkville stopped advertising in Bund newspapers, and by the middle of 1937 the organization's coffers were nearly depleted. A desperate Kuhn had his Bundists scouring the streets of the city for discarded metal, which he sold to junk dealers to raise funds.

In January 1938, with news of Germany's intensified persecution of German Jews, relations between Germany and the United States took another giant step downward. Hitler was now a hair's breadth away from ordering the American Bund out of existence. On February 18, a panicked Kuhn set sail for Germany to plead his case. Meanwhile, in Yorkville plans were underway for a major event. April 20 was Hitler's forty-ninth birthday, and what better way to celebrate the Fuehrer's natal day than to gather a bunch of storm troopers in front of the Yorkville Casino while the Nazis inside spewed their hatred of America's Jews and President Roosevelt?

As the first speaker praised the recent annexation of Austria as a "birthday gift by Chancellor Hitler" to Greater Germany, a riot broke out. Police reinforcements were brought in and before the end of the evening, all of 86th Street between Second and Third avenues was closed off as the rioters spilled into the streets.

One month later, as Congress was about to turn the heat up on the Bund, New York City's Mayor Fiorello La Guardia took a page out of Al Capone's downfall seven years earlier and quietly began to investigate the Bund's finances. All of this pressure only seemed to step up Kuhn's loony

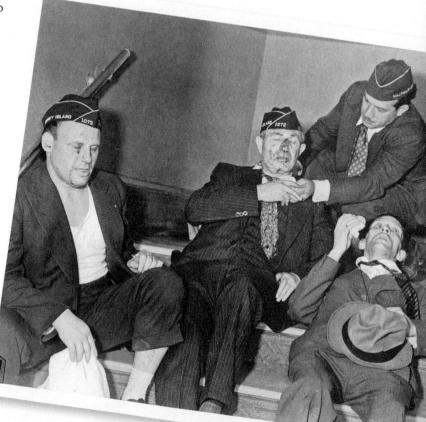

WHEN AMERICAN Legionnaires infiltrated the celebration of Hitler's forty-ninth birthday at the Yorkville Casino on April 20, 1938, several were beaten and sent to hospitals.

Die Ortsgruppe NEW YORK des Bundes

FREUNDE DES NEUEN DEUTSCHLAND

ladet Freunde und Anhänger der Bewegung ein

zur FEIER von

HITLER'S Geburtstag

SAMSTAG, 20. APRIL 1935

ABENDS 8:30 UHR

YORKVILLE CASINO

210 EAST 86th STREET, NEW YORK CITY

Eintritt im Vorverkauf 50c; an der Abendkasse 75c

MILITAERKONZERT der KAPELLE RAPSCH
VORTRAEGE UND DEUTSCHER TANZ

stehen auf dem der **Geburtstagsfreude** und **Fröhlichkeit** gewidmeten **Programm**

Verkaufsstellen: Hindenburg Cafe, 220 East 86th St.
Armbruster's Herrenartikel, 1471 Third Ave., near 83rd St.
Europe Import, 209 East 86th St.
Germania Book Specialty Store, 1517 Dritte Ava.
Cafe Vaterland, 1648 Second Ava., near 86th St.
Franz Sigel's Restaurant, 146 East 85th St.
Bolle & Detzel, 1495 Third Avenue. (84th/85th Str.)

Reimann & Bresse, 1645-1649 Third Avenue. (92nd Str.)
J. Henry Peters, Inc., 217 East 86th Street
Jos. Fischl, 1442 Third Avenue. (82nd Str.)
Elfdende (Bundesleitung), 205 East 85th Street, Room 301
Alfred Haller, Schuhgeerhäft, 1630 First Avenue
Pfälzer Hof, 1611 Second Avenue
Simon Schedler, 657 Teasdaia Place. Bronx

HACKL PRESS, 300 E. 83rd ST., N. Y. C.

A POSTER ANNOUNCING a birthday celebration for Hitler, just two years after he was made chancellor of Germany. The Yorkville Casino was a gathering place and entertainment center for Yorkville's German-American community.

ON NOVEMBER 16, 1938, one week after *Kristallnacht*, these NYU students were promoting a campus meeting to protest concentration camps and persecution of Jews in Germany when they were accosted by a Nazi sympathizer.

behavior. On the sidewalks of New York, his Bundists were handing out lewd pamphlets depicting Jews as sexual perverts. At Bundist meetings in Yorkville's Turnhalle, Kuhn railed against "Jewish Radio," blasting American commentators Walter Winchell, Heywood Broun, and Westbrook Pegler as degenerates. One night when Kuhn entered the Stork Club, Winchell is said to have asked Sherman Billingsley, the club's owner, to hold his pistol lest he be tempted to use it on Kuhn.

Then, on November 9, Hitler's demonic intentions were demonstrated in a well-orchestrated ballet of destruction. That night, more than seven thousand storefront windows of Jewish-owned shops in Germany were smashed and the stores plundered. Synagogues were torched and Jews attacked. *Kristallnacht*, or "The Night of Broken Glass," marked the beginning of the end for Germany's Jews.

President Roosevelt immediately recalled our ambassador as Americans tried to grasp what had occurred. In Manhattan, barely two weeks later, on a mild, overcast night, twenty thousand New Yorkers gathered inside Madison Square Garden, with another two thousand spilling into the streets to hear Dorothy Parker, Dashiell Hammett, and *New York Herald Tribune* reporter Dorothy Thompson attempt to put the country's rage into words. A few blocks west, at Pier 86 where the North German Lloyd liner *Bremen* was due to dock, a group of protesters gathered, hoisting signs that read "Keep Nazi Spy Ships out of New York Harbor" and "Stop Persecution of Protestants, Catholics and Jews in Nazi Germany."

In the same month that Hitler was executing his plan to rid Germany of its Jews, Kuhn was making arrangements for one last shot at telling the American people that they must do the same. Call him crazy, but America's Fuehrer still felt that America had not yet awakened to Hitler's message. He booked Madison Square Garden for a February rally to celebrate the birthday of a national leader. Only it wasn't Hitler's birthday Kuhn was celebrating; it was George Washington's!

New York City's half-Jewish mayor hated the American Bund and Nazi Germany as much as they despised the "Jew *lumpen*." In 1937, he proposed a "Chamber of Horrors" be built for the 1939 World's Fair, depicting all that was evil in Nazi Germany. The Nazi press responded, calling New York City's outspoken mayor a "dirty Talmud Jew." La Guardia knew how to channel his anger, and he never missed an opportunity to use his office as a sharp weapon. When the mayor was instructed by the State Department to provide adequate security for members of the German government and German property, he responded by creating an all-Jewish police detail. Taking a cue from Teddy Roosevelt, who, when he was New York City police commissioner, assigned forty Jewish policemen to guard a visiting anti-Semitic German cleric, La Guardia called on Captain Max Finkelstein from the Greenpoint station in Brooklyn. The man who was president of the department's Shomrim Society would handpick some of his toughest Jewish cops for the detail.

On the Thursday evening of February 20, 1939, seventeen hundred New York City policemen showed up at Eighth Avenue and 50th Street. Four hundred of them were placed inside the Garden, given the odious job of protecting Kuhn and his storm troopers. The rest were outside, some on police horses, trying to hold back the hundreds of New Yorkers who had hoped the event would never have been allowed to take place. "We have enough policemen here to start a revolution," joked Police Commissioner Lewis J. Valentine.

For forty cents, anyone could buy a ticket to Kuhn's strange circus. Inside the Garden, the scene was surreal. Across the stage, four enormous American flags were hung from the ceiling like patriotic drapes. In the center was a thirty-foot-high image of America's first president bathed in an oval of celestial-like light. And just to make sure you understood why you were here, between George Washington and those enormous American flags were equally oversized swastikas. The evening got underway with a procession down the center aisle, of Nazis in storm trooper uniforms carrying more swastikas and American flags. They even sang the "Star-Spangled Banner"!

New York Herald Tribune columnist Dorothy Thompson was jeering and laughing as Kuhn spewed out his anti-Jewish diatribe. Two storm troopers quickly escorted her out. When Isadore Greenbaum from Brooklyn attempted to mount the stage only to be pounced on by a group of Kuhn's men, he made the news. A few days later a Pathé newsreel played the incident at every newsreel theater in Manhattan.

But the real story of that night was happening outside. Crowds filled several city blocks, the din of their anger loud enough to drown out Eighth Avenue's honking taxis. "Drive the Nazis out of New York!" and "Smash anti-Semitism" were just a couple of the signs that were telling the city's bigger story. This was La Guardia's green light to let the hounds loose. On May 25, at 5:45 in the after-

MORE THAN TWENTY THOUSAND NAZI SYMPATHIZERS attended this February 20, 1939, rally at Madison Square Garden. In a bizarre effort to "Americanize" the Bund, an oversized image of George Washington hung center stage, flanked by Nazi flags.

noon, two New York City detectives, together with Joseph Norbury, who was working for District Attorney Thomas E. Dewey, drove up to Schenker's gas station just outside of Krumsville, a Nazi enclave near Allentown, Pennsylvania, and arrested Kuhn. Larceny and embezzlement were the formal charges—specifically the theft of $14,548 of the Bund's funds, money that ironically had come from the

Madison Square Garden rally. New York City's mayor had managed to succeed where Congress had not.

Kuhn's trial was tabloid fodder. Bund money was spent on women, one of whom he had promised to marry, overlooking the fact that he already had a wife. Love letters from "Fritzi" were laughed at over breakfast coffee. But in another country this colorless man would have wiped out lives without a flicker. Fritz Kuhn was the personification of the banality of evil.

On December 5, 1939, Kuhn was sentenced to two and a half years in Sing Sing. The following morning, the "American Fuehrer" was taken from the Tombs in lower Manhattan to Grand Central Terminal, where he would board the 10:30 Albany local to Ossining. Henry Ford, Kuhn's first employer in the United States, happened to be in the terminal waiting for a car that was arriving by freight train. When he learned of Kuhn's presence, Ford went down to Kuhn's train and peered into the car where he sat, handcuffed to one of the seats. Ford said nothing. He merely stared, as if viewing one of Barnum's strange creatures.

In Yorkville people were mostly indifferent to Kuhn's fate. A reporter looking for reaction got shrugged shoulders. At the 86th Street newsstands the only mention of him in any paper was in the *Deutscher Weckruf und Beobachter and the Free American,* the newly named Bund's organ. "Kuhn a Prisoner of War" read the headlines. The Ridder brothers' *New Yorker Staats-Zeitung und Herald*, which had been strangely mute after its original editorial protesting the treatment of Germany's Jews, now openly condemned the Bundists.

Although they managed to hold on until five days before Pearl Harbor, the American Bund was now powerless. Their last meeting, held at Ebling's Casino in the Bronx, didn't even fill the small room. It was the actions of their native country that drove the final nail in the American Bundists' coffin. On September 1, 1939, three months before Kuhn's sentencing, the Nazis invaded Poland. Two days later, Britain and France declared war on Germany. Still, remnants of the Bund would surface, much to the consternation of some New Yorkers. In April 1941, five-year-old Alan Walden accompanied his father to Manhattan, where they were going to visit a friend of his father's who lived in Yorkville. He recalls, "We came out of the 86th Street subway station and everywhere I looked I saw these wonderful red flags. Some of them had white circles, and in the middle of each circle was a strange-looking black cross. I figured it was some sort of celebration." (It was probably a gathering to mark Hitler's birthday.) Walden's father stood frozen in his spot, grabbing his young son's hand in a fierce grip before turning east toward Fifth Avenue, where the pair headed for the Central Park Zoo. His father hardly spoke for the rest of the day.

Eight months later, what was left of the Bund would be scattered to the winds. If New Yorkers were still unsure about where most German-Americans stood it was made crystal clear on December 8, the day after the attack on Pearl Harbor and three days before Germany declared war on the United States. "Our country has been deliberately attacked by Japan, the agent and ally of Nazi Germany," declared the German American Congress for Democracy. The Congress asked all German-Americans to "stand united behind the President and the armed forces of the United States."

The face of Yorkville began to reflect America's reaction to Germany's aggression. At the Garden Theatre, at 158 East 86th Street, German-language movie posters were taken down and the title of the current German film was removed from the marquee. In the neighborhood's beer halls, all signs written in German suddenly disappeared. In German restaurants, "liberty cabbage" was served up instead of sauerkraut. And at 10 East 40th Street, the office of the Board of Trade for German-American Commerce was closed indefinitely. No more *apfelmus* or Bavarian wursts would be coming off German boats. "When the war began all of that pro-German feeling disappeared," says former Yorkville resident Bill Vericker. It took two years before Alan Walden's father sat his son down and broke his silence, explaining his reaction to that April day in Yorkville: "The flags we saw were German flags and Germany is now run by very bad people."

Hollywood felt secure enough of the country's anti-German sentiments to sacrifice a cuddly German dachshund in the 1942 film *All Through the Night*. In the final scene, "Hansel," the doomed Nazi agent's beloved pet, is seen sitting on the explosive-filled boat that will soon turn them both into cinders.

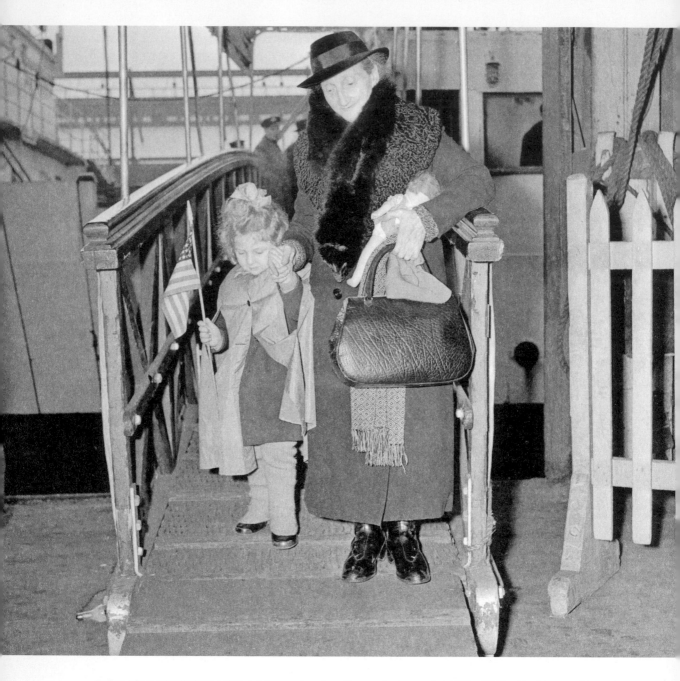

THREE-YEAR-OLD TRUDEL LEVY clutches an American flag as she is escorted off the SS *President Roosevelt* by
Mrs. Emilia Herz. These Jewish refugees arrived in New York City on December 31, 1938.

They're Coming to America!

At that moment, I thought, "Here I am." It was good to be in a new, different world, America, the land of liberty, of freedom.

Werner Kleeman
From Dachau to D-Day

Werner Kleeman was one of the lucky ones. The twenty-one-year old had been arrested by the Nazis shortly after *Kristallnacht* and sent to Dachau. An American cousin came to his aid, depositing money in a London bank, and two months later, in January 1939, Kleeman was released. A visa and a year of saving up for a ticket brought him to New York City on a Friday morning in December 1940. "I got off the boat in New York Harbor and the first thing I did was go into a barbershop with my suitcases to get a haircut," he wrote.

By the time Kleeman set his feet on a New York City sidewalk,

THESE JEWISH REFUGEES
from Germany, Austria, and Czechoslovakia had been
interned in Italy before coming to America. Their eventual destination was an
all-Jewish agrarian colony in the Dominican Republic.

Fritz Kuhn had already served a year in Sing Sing. Still, he and his Bundists had fueled a very real fear in this country of a Fifth Column—Nazis coming here in the guise of refugees—and the immigration quota for German Jews was sharply reduced.

The ones who saw the writing on the wall began arriving in 1933. In the beginning it was just a trickle, mostly artists, writers, university professors, and scientists. They got the message loud and clear on a drizzly night in May, just four months after Hitler became chancellor, when bonfires were lit on university campuses all across Germany. Onto the pyres went the writings of Sigmund Freud, Albert Einstein, Thomas Mann, H. G. Wells, Erich Maria Remarque, and countless others. Einstein's assets were confiscated, after which he immediately renounced his German citizenship. Two months before the first book went up in flames, Jewish physicians were forbidden to work out of Berlin's hospitals, and Jewish judges could no longer hear cases.

These outcasts—some of them world-famous—with the shadow of death behind them sailed into New York Harbor on luxury liners, traveling either first class or tourist, several of them cramming English from guidebooks as they relaxed on deck chairs like any visiting tourist. And when they saw the New York skyline, they, too, rhapsodized.

"When the skyscrapers of Manhattan were stretching out in front of me, I felt almost paralyzed," wrote German actor Walter Wicclair. For writer Joseph Wechsberg, the sight of New York City was an instant addiction: "The trip up the Hudson River, past the skyline of Manhattan, has something overpowering from which no one can withdraw."

But seeing the city from the deck of a luxury liner could be quite different from living and working here. New York City, like the rest of the country, was suffering through the Great Depression, and a walk through Central Park past clusters of shanties dispelled any notions that life here would be easy. There was another problem: with few exceptions, these new emigrants didn't speak English. Martin Gumpert, a well-known writer and a practicing physician in Berlin, wrote, "Ignorant of the language and of the country, penniless and presumptuous, we arrived with our needs and claims in America's moment of crisis."

Bella Fromm, a prominent social reporter in Berlin, landed here on the SS *Normandie* in September 1938. Fromm, who once kept two servants in her Berlin flat where she entertained the city's elite, took a housemaid's job in an East Seventies townhouse, scrubbing pots and washing dishes for the paltry sum of eight dollars a week. The hours were long and the work was not easy. At day's end, she would wait for the midnight bus that delivered her to her dingy furnished room, her aching feet bringing tears to her eyes. "But I was happy," she later wrote. "I was doing all right; doing much better, even, than I had thought I would."

Some refugees tried to reinvent themselves, enrolling in courses like the ones the National Refugee Service offered in the Times Square area where they were trained to become mechanics. But for many professionals, especially the intellectuals who had enjoyed high esteem in Germany, it was deeply humiliating to be reduced to menial work. "We thought we had much to give and soon saw ourselves more helpless than beggars, because we were not used to begging," wrote Martin Gumpert.

Professors not fortunate enough to be hired by a university found themselves on job lines, competing with out-of-work New Yorkers for dishwasher jobs. Writers took jobs as messengers and fur packers. A few became janitors. Lawyers worked in garment center factories, cutting fabric. Opera composer Paul Dessau took a job on a New Jersey chicken farm. Physician and writer Richard Berczeller delivered groceries. And writer Hans Natonek, who got a job as a hospital worker, was carrying a corpse to the dissection lab of a New York City hospital when he got a call from his literary agent informing him that his autobiography had found a publisher. Medical doctors had to take a New York State medical exam, a daunting experience when they could neither read nor write in English. And how would they converse with non–German-speaking patients? It was not easy. For many, there were memories of first nights in flophouses, or a daily diet of apples until a job came up. One young man employed as an errand boy in a flower shop saved the nickel carfare he was given so he could get a meal.

Those who would not or could not support themselves with menial jobs often relied on spouses, since housekeeping positions always seemed to be available. In her novel *Die Engel*, based on her own experiences, Bella Fromm's female character says of emigrant wives, "They

PASSENGERS ARRIVING IN NEW YORK HARBOR on the *Queen Mary* gather on deck at dawn to see the city's famous skyline. This 1939 crossing was one of the ocean liner's last before she was converted to a troopship.

cleaned offices, they worked, as I did, in a factory. They became housekeepers or cooks, and if luck was with them, they got a housekeeper's position with room and bath where their husbands could live in with them. If he was capable of being a butler, all the better; then the pay was increased. If this was not the case, the women simply gritted their teeth and made it possible for the former bank directors or academicians to relearn their professions here or to let themselves be retrained in order to eventually earn their own wages."

For the famous ones, many of whom already lived nomadic lives, the transition could be easier. Conductors Otto Klemperer and Bruno Walter signed up with American orchestras before setting sail. Bertolt Brecht, Kurt Weill, and Arnold Schoenberg had artistic reputations that preceded them. Some of the fortunate scholars and scientists whose credentials were recognized here were able to continue their work. Both Columbia University and the New School for Social Research invited German-Jewish scholars to teach and continue their research. Columbia became the new home for the Frankfurt School of Social Research, while the New School funded a "University in Exile" for social science professors whose teachings were no longer permitted in Nazi Germany.

The one thing all refugees, lucky and unlucky, could count on, the one thing that gave them some joy, was New York City. With its large Jewish population, the city was not a bad place to end up. Where once they congregated in the Bohemian cafés of Berlin and Vienna, they now hung out in the Deauville restaurant on East 73rd Street or in the Café Éclair across Central Park on West 72nd Street. The Cafe Éclair became such a well-known gathering place for German and Austrian refugees, the more famous ones scribbled messages in a leather-bound guest book that has been carefully preserved. On the Lower East Side, they would attend a play at one of a string of theaters that made up the Jewish Rialto and discuss it over coffee and strudel at the Café Royal on Second Avenue and 12th Street. The café was a favorite meeting place for the playwrights and actors who worked in the Yiddish theater.

Many of them settled on the Upper West Side, referred to in the 1930s as the "gilded ghetto" because it was home to most of the city's wealthy and upper-middle-class Jews. The fortunate ones shared space with family or friends who had large apartments on Central Park West or West End Avenue. Others ended up in mid-block rooming houses or cheap hotels like the Milburn or the Marseilles, taking their meals in local coffee shops or at the Horn & Hardart Automat on Broadway and 72nd Street or the one at 104th. The new immigrants loved the automat because the famous vending machine walls had food in full view. All that was required to release the little glass doors were a few nickels. No English was required to get a meal. "There you could get by mutely," wrote Fritz Stern, who was twelve years old when his parents brought him here. "You dropped a nickel . . . in a slot and out came a sandwich or a slice of pie."

In some ways, Broadway with its old-world apartment buildings and its bustling shops reminded these transplanted urbanites of Vienna and Berlin. They would sit on benches along the tree-lined traffic islands that divide Broadway and read copies of *Aufbau*, the house organ of the German Jewish Club on West 91st Street. The twelve-page newsletter, published in German, offered advice on how to cope in this new city. They could get a nosh at Steinberg's, the kosher dairy restaurant on Broadway and 81st Street. "We all found each other," says Vienna-born Lily Hollander, who was ten years old when she arrived with her parents and moved into a five-story walk-up on 82nd Street between Amsterdam and Columbus avenues. "We gave parties at home and shared certain recipes. One of them was 'refugee goulash,' made with frankfurters and potatoes and lots of paprika." Lily's mother tried to supplement the family's meager earnings by opening a Viennese bakery, which failed within a year. "There were a lot of Viennese bakeries," Lily remembers. "Most did not last."

On the other side of town, the Y.M.H.A. on the Upper East Side provided dormitory space for refugees, teaching them English and counseling them in the ways of their new city. Some settled into apartments in the more suburban Queens enclaves of Forest Hills and Jackson Heights, a seemingly odd choice since ads for the Jackson Heights garden apartment complex posted on Fifth Avenue buses let it be known that they were restricted and did not allow Jews.

The one part of Manhattan where the new arrivals could feel completely at home was Washington Heights. This narrow sliver of upper Manhattan bounded by the Hudson and Harlem rivers and filled with block after block of low-rise brick apartment buildings was known now by the nicknames "Frankfurt on the Hudson" and "The Fourth Reich," because it had the largest concentration of German-Jews in the entire country. German was more common on the streets than English. Lining the avenues were delis specializing in German-Jewish food, German bakeries, and kosher butcher shops. Lublo's Palm Garden, a German cabaret, featured German-Jewish entertainment. And because the neighborhood was more small village than cosmopolitan city, it attracted not writers and artists, but lawyers, doctors, and businessmen. Washington Heights was a place for professionals who were not necessarily intellectuals.

Being able to speak in their native tongue made life for those who settled in Washington Heights a good deal easier. But even in this German-speaking enclave the new refugees encountered problems. When Lily Hollander's family moved there, they enrolled her in the neighborhood school. She recalls, "Some of the children—boys especially—would yell 'Heil Hitler!' when we passed. It was the language of the enemy." Klaus Mann, son of writer Thomas Mann, was carrying on a conversation with his sister, Erika, in a Manhattan bar when a man sitting near them suddenly stood up and shouted, "I can't stand it! That damned Nazi talk! That filthy gibberish! Stop it! Shut up! Or speak English!" Once the United States was at war with Germany, *Aufbau* was one of several German-language newspapers that cautioned their readers not to speak German in public.

All of this was ironic in light of the one obstacle that took the new immigrants by surprise. Like the rest of the country, New York City was not immune to anti-Semitism. Herbert H. Lehman, a German Jew, may have been governor, and the half-Jewish Fiorello La Guardia the city's mayor, but Jews couldn't live in certain apartment buildings (including some that they built!) or in certain neighborhoods. Jack Gold, who grew up on Amsterdam Avenue and 100th Street—an Irish working-class neighborhood—was threatened by an Italian barber who told him, "Mussolini's gonna take care of you!" Even in predominantly Jewish Washington Heights there was a group of upscale English Tudor apartments that didn't take Jews. And Jews looking in the want ads would come across quite a few "Christians only" notices. Kathryn

Gibbs, the prestigious secretarial school, would not enroll Jewish women because they couldn't place them in jobs. It was one thing to visit a bar in Yorkville and risk a bloody nose if certain people discovered your ethnicity, but to know that Columbia, the university that opened its doors to exiled German-Jewish scholars, would keep those same doors shut to so many Jewish students was mystifying.

Equally mystifying to the new immigrants was the general complacence among New Yorkers to Hitler's looming threat. True, as early as May 1933, just days after Germany's infamous book burning, every Jewish-owned store in New York closed its doors as 100,000 New York Jews and Christians marched from Madison Square to the Bowery, denouncing Hitler's persecution of Germany's Jews. Three months later, while locked in a crippling Depression, the City of New York pledged one million dollars to a fund to get Jews out of Germany. But these were isolated acts in a city that had yet to grasp the reach of Hitler's ambitions. Bella Fromm, who was pursued in New York by Gestapo agents intent on killing her, wrote in *Blood and Banquets: A Berlin Social Diary*, "It was almost shocking to see that, except intellectually, the Nazi danger was still not realized in the United States . . . Most people were completely ignorant of the new psychology in Germany, that of a mind gone berserk, a nation shouting too loudly and too insanely to hear the voice of reason . . ."

On her first visit in the summer of 1935—three years before she came here to live—Fromm was at the dock where the SS *Berlin* was berthed, watching aghast as eighty German-American members of the Steuben Society who were guests of the Third Reich boarded the ship. She wrote, "It was hard to believe my eyes. Neatly drawn up on the pier in military formation was a battalion of Storm Troopers. Black trousers, the loathsome high boots, the swastika band around the right sleeve of the brown shirt. Arms were raised. Heels clicked. The Nazi flag, coupled with the Stars and Stripes, flapping insolently in the free air."

Playwright Bertolt Brecht decided to do something about it. Together with a group of German and Austrian intellectuals, Brecht produced *We Fight Back*, a radio series providing political discourse from the exiles' point of view. Shortwave radio got their message into Nazi-occupied countries. In June of 1934, Nobel Prize–winning German novelist Thomas Mann addressed seventy-five American writers at the Author's Club on West 76th Street, urging them to take up the fight against the "power of darkness." In the 1940s, Mann's radio speeches would be transmitted from New York to London, where the BBC then broadcast them into Central Europe.

By 1939, *Aufbau*, the little service-oriented newsletter, had become the voice of the German-Jewish exiles in America. During the war years, both Thomas Mann and Albert Einstein contributed articles and Hannah Arendt wrote a regular column. Helmut F. Pfanner considered it "the most important rallying point of German and Austrian intellectuals in America and, perhaps, throughout the world."

A year later, German political exiles in New York City convinced America's labor unions to form the Emergency Rescue Committee. German and Austrian Jews still trapped in occupied France needed to be rescued. In August 1940 the committee sent foreign correspondent Varian Fry to Marseilles. Fry helped rescue thousands, among them artists Marc Chagall, Max Ernst, and André Breton. Once the United States entered the war, there would be another major outlet for German-speaking intellectuals eager to spread the word about Hitler's atrocities. In 1942 the Office of War Information was formed. This propaganda arm of the government, which produced newsreels, several pro-American radio series, and the Voice of America, was a perfect match for them.

THESE CHILDREN GREETING THE STATUE OF LIBERTY were among a group of fifty Jewish refugees from Vienna who were placed with foster families in Philadelphia. Fear of inflaming American anti-Semitism prevented sponsors of the *kindertransport* from openly publicizing their efforts.

Meanwhile, New Yorkers continued to try to help Jews still in Germany. On November 9, 1934, nine German Jews arrived in New York Harbor. What made this small group so unusual was the fact that they were all young boys, ranging in age from eleven to fourteen, and with the exception of the man who accompanied them across the ocean, they were alone. On this first trip, the Jewish-American organizations that put this *kindertransport* into operation had hoped to bring 250 youngsters from Hitler's Germany, but fear of spiking the city's anti-Semitism and possibly sabotaging the project made it difficult for them to advertise. By the time American Jews got the word either in their synagogues or through word of mouth, only nine families qualified to take in the children. It would be very different for British children sent here during the Blitz a few years later. Arriving with a great deal of publicity, they were welcomed with open arms.

By 1941, *Kristallnacht* had made the United States well aware of Nazi atrocities, and larger groups of Jewish boys and girls were coming in and being sent to foster homes throughout the country. Faced with the grim reality of what was in store for them in Nazi Germany, the children who arrived were very resilient and, for the most part, anxious to begin their new lives here. Trudy Kirchhausen was fourteen years old when, in 1938, the SS *Hamburg* brought her to New York City: "The morning we sailed into the harbor of New York and saw the Statue of Liberty, I cheered loud and clear and knew that I was going to this new home free from fear and destruction." Before Germany was defeated, the *kindertransport* would deliver one thousand Jewish children to America.

One of the most unusual rescue efforts was started not in the United States but in Germany by a well-known German manufacturer. In 1933, Ernst Leitz, head of Germany's famous Leica camera company, was approached by some of his Jewish business associates. They needed to get their families out of Germany quickly. Could Leitz help? In no time, Leitz became the photography industry's Oskar Schindler, sending some of his new "employees" to New York City. Disembarking from the SS *Bremen* with Leica cameras around their necks, these Jews, who were part of what became known as the "Leica Freedom Train," made their way to the company's Manhattan headquarters, where they were given jobs.

To their great surprise, most of these reluctant immigrants would make New York City their true home. Artists particularly loved the city's energy and the constant friction between the beautiful and the ugly. Klaus Mann "knew right

away, when we rode from the harbor to the Astor Hotel." With his twin sister, he "roved from Harlem to Wall Street; from Chinatown to the German district; from Central Park to Brooklyn; from the Bronx to the Village," captured "by the rhythm and blast of this new splendor . . ." Composer Kurt Weill and his wife, singer Lotte Lenya, felt the same way. Weill loved to wander the city streets for inspiration. He became American almost immediately, writing his first American musical, *Knickerbocker Holiday*, with Maxwell Anderson in 1938, based on Washington Irving's *History of New York*. It was followed by *Lady in the Dark*, which he wrote with Moss Hart and Ira Gershwin in 1941, and *One Touch of Venus* two years later. Once America went to war with Germany, Weill signed on for *Lunch-Hour Follies*, the American Theatre Wing's effort to entertain workers in war plants and factories all around the city. Weill performed when he could (as an alien he was often not permitted in factories), serenading the workers with his composition "Buddy on the Nightshift." Martin Gumpert knew he was a real New Yorker when he realized that whenever he had to leave the city he became "homesick for the infernal noise of Second Avenue."

These reluctant émigrés gave back generously to the city and the country that took them in. Director Erwin Piscator's Dramatic Workshop, which had its origins in the New School, would draw the talents of Tennessee Williams, Arthur Miller, Marlon Brando, Tony Curtis, and Harry Belafonte. Viennese-born Otto Preminger, who worked with the legendary director Max Reinhardt in Germany until Reinhardt was forced to leave Berlin, played Nazis in Hollywood films before becoming a director himself. Movies were made from the novels of Vicki Baum (*Grand Hotel*) and Erich Maria Remarque (*All Quiet on the Western Front* and *Bobby Deerfield*).

As for the children who came here with the *kindertransport*, many of them certainly did their adoptive country proud. Jack Steinberger, who was sent to America with his brother in 1934, won the Nobel Prize in Physics in 1988 for his work in the discovery of new subatomic particles. Another eleven-year-old who grew up with a foster family here became a legendary impresario of American music, launch-ing the careers of Otis Redding, Jefferson Airplane, and the Grateful Dead. Born Wolfgang Grajonca in Berlin, he was best known to American audiences as Bill Graham.

Once Germany declared war on the United States, some of those children were old enough to enlist in the U.S. Armed Forces and did. If they had gone to the recruiting office in Times Square, they might have run into Klaus Mann. The man who rhapsodized over his adopted city did what most young New York men did when he learned his new country was at war: he joined the army. As an enemy alien, Werner Kleeman could not enlist. Instead he waited to be called up. In August 1942 the letter of induction arrived, and the man who escaped one of Hitler's concentration camps became part of the D-Day invasion. When the war was over, Kleeman got his own revenge when he helped arrest the man who sent him to Dachau.

THE MAJESTIC *QUEEN ELIZABETH* slipped quietly into New York Harbor on March 7, 1940. Fearing an attack by German U-boats, the luxury liner's maiden voyage was kept secret. Like her sister ship, *Queen Mary*, she would soon be fitted as a troopship.

The Lull Before the Storm

"Bob, you ought to see what's going on up in the salon. People are sobbing. One woman stopped me and said there are German submarines waiting for the order to sink this ship."

Dolores Hope to Bob Hope onboard the SS *Queen Mary*,
Southhampton to New York, September 4, 1939

The tugboat *Eugene F. Moran* was the first to spot her at 9:52 that morning. Captain Walter Clark described a "speck" moving up the channel as she cut through the blue-gray haze. Gradually she began to take form, a hulking gray mass like some enormous sea ghost looming against the pale sky. At ten minutes to eleven, the breathtaking form of the SS *Queen Elizabeth* approached Quarantine, the Public Health Station off Rosebank, Staten Island. By now, a flotilla of small craft should have been sailing toward her, ready to accompany her for the final stretch of her journey into New York Harbor. Where were the fireboats welcoming her with sprays of Hudson River water, the way they had the *Normandie* in 1935 and the *Queen Mary* a year later? Where was the band at the Battery and the crowds of cheering New Yorkers who always lined up along the Brooklyn shoreline for a momentous maritime event?

This was, after all, the maiden voyage of Britain's brand-new, much-anticipated super liner, the largest, fastest, most luxurious passenger ship in the world. The *Queen Elizabeth* had been christened two years before by Princesses Elizabeth and Margaret, but a year later, on the day she was due to be launched, Britain declared war against Germany and the British fleet was mobilized. Now, with the war intensifying, Britain's brand-new luxury liner was a sitting target, a tempting invitation to the German Luftwaffe to come and get her. What was to be done with her?

On February 26, 1940, without any fanfare, the newest ocean queen slipped quietly out of her berth in Clydeside, Scotland's famous shipyard, her stately interiors stripped of furnishings and the windows on her Promenade Deck blacked out with paint. She carried no passengers, just a crew of slightly under four hundred, and no one on board including her captain was informed of her final destination until the ship was in open waters.

In the winter of 1940 German submarines infested the Atlantic Ocean, seeking out British merchant and naval vessels, their aim to destroy the entire British fleet and starve Britain. They did not yet venture beyond the middle of the ocean under instructions from Hitler, who was playing for time, hoping the United States was not going to involve itself in his war with Britain. Still, German submarines were everywhere, and right now, their sights would certainly be trained on the new *Queen Elizabeth*. If their subs and the mines didn't get her, perhaps the Luftwaffe would.

A convoy escorted her during her first day at sea until she was safely away from Britain, but the four-day trip across the treacherous Atlantic was hers to make alone. And because her voyage was a secret, no one on the other side of the ocean knew when to expect her. It was not until 6:00 on the night of March 6 that she was spotted off the coast of Nantucket and Western Union towers at Quarantine near Sandy Hook began looking out for her. At the West 47th Street police station, Chief Inspector Louis Costuma ordered one hundred extra patrolmen and detectives and ten mounted police to show up at Cunard's Pier 90 at 6:00 the following morning. The police were here to protect the ship as she slid into her berth next to her sister ship, the *Queen Mary*, and the Cunard's *Mauritania*, a favorite of former Mayor Jimmy

COMEDIAN BOB HOPE AND HIS WIFE, Dolores, were passengers on the *Queen Mary*'s last civilian crossing when they left England on August 30, 1939. On September 4, when the ship was en route to America, England declared war on Germany. After evading German U-boats, the ocean liner arrived safely in New York Harbor.

storm swept across the Hudson River, passengers on the Weehawken ferry watched as the two liners stealthily made their way out to sea. Stripped of their luxurious appointments, they had become part of a fleet of troop transports, to be joined later by the *Queen Elizabeth*.

In November 1939, Congress passed the Neutrality Act, effectively establishing a "count-us-out" policy as Britain, France, Australia, and Canada went to war with Germany. But once the war began depriving Britain of badly needed fuel oil and vital supplies, the United States realized it had to step in to help. To circumvent the country's non-intervention policy, President Roosevelt signed the Lend-Lease Act into law in March 1941, giving the United States the green light to supply

Walker, which had remained in New York Harbor since the outbreak of war.

On March 18, just eleven days after the *Queen Elizabeth* slipped into New York Harbor, 770 British seamen arrived here on Cunard's White Star liner *Antonia*. Three hundred of them immediately boarded the *Mauritania* and the others went onto the *Queen Mary*, which had been hastily given a second, darker coat of gray paint. Two nights later as a rain-

NEW YORKERS AT A TIMES SQUARE NEWSSTAND as newspaper headlines announce the beginning of war in Europe. Americans were willing to help England and France, but they stood behind the Neutrality Act, passed two months later, which made it clear that the United States would not go to war with Germany.

England and other Allied nations with vital war materials in exchange for the use of their military bases. Even before that legislation, the needs of England were being addressed. In the early spring of 1940, the reconditioned *Panamanian*, a cargo-passenger liner that had been rusting for five years on the New Jersey waterfront, set sail for Britain loaded with supplies.

That same month, President Roosevelt, fearing what was coming, began pressing for the upgrade of the country's waterways and harbors. The U.S. Navy prepared to stretch heavy nets across major harbors, protecting them against German torpedoes, mines, and the deadly submarines. It was even suggested, as a defense against invasion, that a 1,000-acre island be built in New York Harbor south of Governor's Island out of landfill from the Brooklyn Battery Tunnel. New York City was urged to deepen the East River channel all the way from the Upper Bay, past the Brooklyn Navy Yard to Throgs Neck, so that the navy's largest warships could pass between New York Harbor and Long Island Sound. By September 1940, President Roosevelt asked that a super dry dock be constructed in New York Harbor to handle the 45,000-ton battleships under construction in the Brooklyn Navy Yard. This war that isolationists kept saying had nothing to do with us appeared to be getting closer.

As the war in Europe intensified, ships that had been bringing refugees to New York City were now carrying Americans who were told that it was no longer safe for them to remain in Europe. By the end of May 1940, diplomats were sending their wives and children home. Julia Marlowe, a former actress returning to New York on the United States liner SS *Washington*, claimed she could hear the guns from her summer home in Lausanne, Switzerland.

On her ship was Dorothy Thompson, the *New York Herald-Tribune* reporter who had observed first hand what was happening in Europe. "I think we should go into this struggle," she said. "There is no question that the Nazis are contemplating the worst fate for England."

On June 14, the Germans entered Paris. Now the German air force had the ability to strike from bases in occupied France, rendering British convoys in the English Channel sitting ducks. By July, Nazi planes and U-boats were devastating Britain's ships, and everyone knew there was much more to come.

New York Harbor was now a player in this deadly war game. In late July, the army placed a string of dummy mines at the mouth of the harbor near the New Jersey shore as part of a practice maneuver. Warships were as common a sight in the Hudson River as luxury liners had been. Just a month before, on June 11, the bombed and battered Holland-America Line's SS *Delftdijk* arrived here from Holland, its twenty-one passengers telling chilling stories of dodging Nazi planes as they were put to work sealing windows and hastily camouflaging the ship with a coat of muddy orange paint. That same month, Italy declared war on France and Britain. Italian liners arriving here were regularly searched before their cargo could be offloaded. Along the Brooklyn

MAYOR LA GUARDIA
pastes a "Defend Your Country" poster on a Railway Express
truck as part of a campaign to enlist New Yorkers into the armed forces.

waterfront, Italian-American longshoremen were carefully screened before being allowed to load British ships. New Yorkers looking up in the sky might spot one of the U.S. Navy's surveillance planes, identified by white stars on their wings, flying low over approaching merchant ships.

By July's end, as the war in Europe continued to rage, U.S. diplomats were being called home. New York Harbor was busy with arrivals of the SS *Manhattan*, the SS *Washington*, and the

SS *Excalibur*. Every day, ships would dock at the city's piers from Liverpool, Lisbon, Finland, and Greece, depositing more Americans and refugees. As the German air force was starting its bombing campaign against parts of England—the prelude to its massive blitzkrieg—Britain's House of Commons made an unusual plea to the United States: *Please take the children!* With available places for them in the British countryside becoming scarce, there were few alternatives. The idea worried President Roosevelt. What if one of those baby-filled ships was sunk by the Germans while crossing the Atlantic? The United States could suddenly find itself in the middle of the war. First Lady Eleanor Roosevelt had already started the ball rolling, however, and by the time Congress got around to okaying the use of American ships for the children's evacuation, thousands of British children were assigned to American homes, thanks to the U.S. Committee for the Care of European Children.

Their journey across the mine-filled Atlantic could be frightening, but New York City managed to put a smile

AUGUST 14, 1940. Mayor La Guardia, in Times Square, promotes an Army recruitment campaign. Exactly one month later, President Roosevelt signed the Selective Service and Training Act, requiring all males between the ages of twenty-one and thirty to register for the draft.

BRITISH CHILDREN
sent to America were able to speak
to their parents via shortwave radio across three thousand miles
of U-boat–infested ocean as part of the "Friendship Bridge" program.

on their little faces, providing a welcome diversion as the young refugees waited to be sent to foster homes across the country. Times Square was "just as it is in the films," said one boy. The sight of New York traffic with the city's famous speeding taxis amazed all of the children. They were astounded that the city was not blacked out at night. One seven-year-old particularly liked New York because he saw so many airplanes and none were dropping bombs. British-born actress Angela Lansbury was fourteen years old when she arrived in New York City on the *Duchess of Atholl*: "We were very worried about U-boats on the way over. It was hairy. Our ship was actually sunk on its way back to England." Lansbury, who arrived here with her mother and brother, felt the same way about the city as other transplanted Britons: "New York was incredible. The taxis had glass roofs. You could sail down the streets and look up at the skyscrapers. I always remember that Coca-Cola tasted so wonderful."

If New York provided a temporary harbor for the children of Britain, it also rose to the needs of those who remained behind. Even before the Blitz, Londoners were facing a cold winter with little heat. In early January 1940, Natalie Wales Latham, a young New York society matron, had an idea. Convincing the owner of a vacant Park Avenue store to allow her and some friends to use it rent-free, she bought a box of wool yarn and distributed the wool among the other society women who joined her at the store. One of the ladies drew a rough sketch of a sailor on a trawler and taped it to the window. The women sat in the store all day knitting gloves, socks, and the beginnings of a few sweaters for the British soldiers, sailors, and airmen fighting on the frigid North Sea. They were hoping their visibility would encourage other women strolling along the avenue to join in. Mrs. Latham had hit upon something. By night's end, the small shop was jammed with knitters.

On January 14, 1940, six days after England began nationwide rationing, Bundles for Britain was launched. The idea was simple: Any woman in the city who found herself with an hour or two to spare and the ability to purl some wool or stitch a seam could drop into the store and put her talents to work for a vital cause. By year's end, Natalie Latham's cottage charity reached far beyond New York City, with 270 chapters throughout the country. The small Park Avenue shop had metamorphosed into a suite of offices in the Squibb Building on upper Fifth Avenue. The items were packed and shipped in another building on West 89th Street. They had expanded

SOCIETY MATRON NATALIE Wales Latham began 'Bundles for Britain' modestly by forming a knitting circle in a store window, where women made sweaters and scarves for bombed-out Londoners.

like Bundles for Britain. Grant, who has a funny scene in which he perfects his knitting skills, is said to have donated his salary for the movie (as well as for *The Philadelphia Story*) to British War Relief.

to include everything from gloves and scarves to surgical instruments, x-ray machines, and operating tables.

Bundles for Britain became so much a part of the world-at-war scene in America, it was the inspiration for the 1943 film *Mr. Lucky*, in which gambler Cary Grant falls for Laraine Day, a society woman working for a war relief organization much

Years before *Mr. Lucky* was released, Broadway was on the job with its own war relief efforts. In January 1940, just four months after Britain declared war on Germany, Gertrude Lawrence and Antoinette Perry formed the American Theatre Wing of Allied Relief, using their show-biz visibility to spread the word. They had their own sewing room in their Fifth Avenue headquarters, filled not with society matrons but with the kind of high-profile celebrities one might find in a Hirschfeld drawing. They also hawked souvenirs—makeup compacts, cigarette cases, and autographed programs bearing the British War Relief Society insignia—in theater lobbies, but it was Vivien Leigh's face on the cover of *Look* magazine, a pair of knitting needles in her beautiful hands, that put the war relief programs on the national map.

By January 1941, relief efforts were in high gear. Four months before, on September 7 at 4:56 in the evening, all of London was frozen in the deathly glow of Hitler's Lightning War. In one horrific night. 430 Londoners were killed and sixteen hundred wounded, and that was just the beginning. The nightly devastation would continue until late spring. Every college in New York City was soon raising money for ambulances, which were sent to England. Wall Street joined in, as did the city's physicians and surgeons who helped gather

all kinds of medical supplies, from blood transfusion equipment to cots for London's wounded. Checks to fuel the ambulances and run the hospitals were getting larger as London's civilian casualties grew. When London's Royal Northern Hospital was bombed, it was "adopted" by Bundles for Britain and a check for $10,000 was quickly dispatched. Within a month, the number of bombed London hospitals adopted by Bundles for Britain would grow to nineteen and by April, when the capital experienced its most deadly air raid, that number would climb to 165, nearly all of the city's hospitals.

As the needs of the British intensified, women would meet arriving British freighters that were here to collect donated steel and fill the sailors' arms with scarves, gloves, and sweaters. City schoolchildren collected money and donated their outgrown clothing. Concerts were held at Carnegie Hall, and in May, some of the city's finest stores—Bonwit Teller, Bergdorf Goodman, Henri Bendel, Russeks, DePinna, and Arnold Constable—held a "Buy Something British" week, stocking their stores

ADS FOR 'BUNDLES FOR BRITAIN' appeared everywhere, even inside matchbook covers.

Help England To-day—
Say "I'm glad I did" instead of "I wish I had"
Bundles for Britain, Inc.
745 FIFTH AVENUE
NEW YORK CITY
Enclosed find my contribution for $_____
Name_____
Address_____
City_____ State_____
(DETACH MATCHES BEFORE MAILING)

BUNDLES
FOR
BRITAIN

ARTIST GRANT WOOD PAINTED *BLITZKRIEG!* in 1940 for 'Bundles for Britain.' This poster, depicting a mother shielding her child from Nazi bombers, was an emotional plea for aid to England. *Art copyright Estate of Grant Wood. Licensed by VAGA, New York, NY.*

with British products and posting signs in their display windows. By March, fifty trucks left Bundles for Britain's warehouse on West 89th Street with nearly two thousand boxes of clothing, blankets, and medical supplies, by far the largest shipment yet.

In June, as the case against Germany continued to gather steam, New Yorkers could file into the lobby of the Hollywood Theatre on Broadway and 51st Street to see the German Messerschmitt that had been shot down over London presented to Bundles for Britain. Brooklynites who had held their own "Brooklyn for Britain Week" could catch a glimpse of the plane when it was brought to Coney Island's Luna Park.

Not everyone in New York City was anxious to help the Brits. In September 1940, America First, an aggressive movement to keep the United States out of the European war, snared Charles Lindbergh, the flyer who had once been the country's Golden Boy. Lindbergh not only believed that the war between Germany and Britain was a fratricidal one, he was an admirer of Germany and had entertained living there after his son's kidnapping. One of his prized possessions was a Service Cross of the Order of the German Eagle, studded with swastikas and given to him by Field Marshal Hermann Goering. The famous flyer toured the country for America First, delivering speech after speech on non-intervention. His appearance in April 1941 at Manhattan Center on 34th Street, where he protested the use of U.S. Naval convoys to protect British supply ships, drew praise from a Nazi newspaper in Berlin and a virulent attack from Mayor La Guardia. By October, when he was back in New York City for another, much larger antiwar rally at Madison Square Garden, his aversion to President Roosevelt, Jews, and the British was no secret. In April, the aviator's controversial political stand had forced him to resign his position in the U.S. Army Air Corps Reserve. But that didn't deter the twenty thousand New Yorkers opposed to the United States getting into the war from showing up to cheer him on.

What Lindbergh and the America First group didn't know was that whenever they held a rally, planted in their audience were Brits to derail their movement. The plants were Winston Churchill's idea. In June 1940, England was heavily invested in the United States, a country that was not in the war and under no obligation to protect British interests. Fearing sabotage from German spies already in this country, Churchill sent William Stephenson to New York City to make sure England's vital resources here were secure. The Canadian millionaire set up his headquarters in room 3603 on the thirty-sixth floor of Rockefeller Center with the innocuous title of British Passport Control Officer on the door. Stephenson was in fact a master spy, heading up Britain's secret intelligence network throughout the Western Hemisphere. One of his assignments was to help convince the American people that Britain's war with Germany was their war as well. Defusing the isolationists was part of that plan. Influencing the media was another. Stephenson is said to have persuaded columnists Walter Winchell and Drew Pearson to write items sympathizing with Britain's plight. Stephenson would become a close advisor to FDR, suggesting he put his good friend Bill Donovan in charge of the fledgling U.S. intelligence services, which would become the CIA.

Stephenson went under the code name INTREPID, and his reputation as a man obsessed with his job was well known. Author Ian Fleming, who was working for British Naval Intelligence when Stephenson was installed in his Rockefeller Center office, was, according to Jennet Conant (*The Irregulars: Roald Dahl and the British Spy Ring in Wartime Washington*), given a rare opportunity to observe Stephenson's crew in action. On a summer evening in 1941, Fleming accompanied them on a staged break-in of the Japanese consul general's office, conveniently located just two floors below Stephenson's in Rockefeller Center.

After gaining entry with the help of a janitor, Stephenson's men "managed to crack the safe and make microfilm copies of the codebooks, which contained ciphers the Japanese had been using to transmit messages to Tokyo by shortwave radio. Before morning, everything in the safe was returned to its exact place, and there was no sign they had ever been there." In his first James Bond thriller, Fleming, who was fascinated by Stephenson's gadgets, particularly his ciphering machines (used to decode foreign messages), has Bond shoot a Japanese cipher expert at Rockefeller Center. He would later write that while Bond was a highly romanticized spy, William Stephenson was the real thing.

Even before Stephenson set up shop here, fears were growing in New York City that the German air force that had devastated London could soon cross the Atlantic, imperiling American cities up and down the coast. In February 1940, Mayor La Guardia, who had been given the job of heading the Office of Civilian Defense for the entire nation, issued a warning to mayors in East and West Coast cities, alerting them to the possibility of German air attacks. Knowing that his city would be a prime target, the mayor believed it was imperative that New York City begin taking steps to protect itself. On June 30, he gathered the zone leaders of the city's volunteer air-raid wardens together with police, fire, and city officials to discuss what needed to be done should New York City find itself under attack. In addition to 62,000 air-raid wardens, the mayor was asking for 28,000 specially trained volunteers to manually turn off the city lights in the event of a blackout. A fire auxiliary force was already being trained, and volunteer "spotters"—who would remain on rooftops should enemy planes attack—were being canvassed.

On a Saturday in November at 2:15 in the afternoon, simultaneous bombs went off in each of the five boroughs. In Manhattan, the first attack took place at Union Square just as a second was going off in Brooklyn's Borough Hall, a third at the County Courthouse in the Bronx, a fourth at 168th Street and Hillside Avenue in Queens, and a fifth in the Richmond Borough Hall on Staten Island. Minutes later, another attack occurred in Manhattan, this time at Pier 87 where the *Normandie* was berthed. Mayor La Guardia, who was at the Union Square bombing, raced uptown with his police escort in a record nine minutes, just as his volunteer auxiliary fire department was putting out the fire. The bombs were nothing more than magnesium flares and sulfur pots, part of a mock attack using all of the city's seventy thousand volunteers. The staged bombings intrigued New Yorkers, who celebrated them with a series of impromptu parades. But they were also a clear indication of the importance the mayor was placing on defending the city against an attack.

In early May, the mayor put New York Harbor's entire defense system on alert when he ordered a mock attack on three "enemy submarines." Five thousand soldiers from Fort Tilden in Queens and New Jersey's Fort Hancock manned their guns as the mythical German subs approached. The drill was in response to a February report out of London indicating that the number of German U-boats in the Atlantic had quadrupled and were now traveling in "wolf packs," inflicting maximum damage on convoys. That month the smaller U-boats had sunk thirteen British freighters, including several ocean liners, picking them off like ducks in a shooting gallery.

National defense was now on the minds of most New Yorkers, at times taking precedence over the need to aid their Allies. As summer approached, the ladies who chaired the society functions in the Hamptons were now raising funds for the USO and the American Red Cross. In June, a "Women in National Defense" drive was held at the Plaza Hotel, recruiting women who wanted to learn to fly. By October, all American males between the ages of twenty-one and twenty-five were required to register for the draft.

In the summer of 1940, Congress had budgeted over $8 billion for battleships and bombers, and now, a year later, aluminum was needed to build them. In July 1941, a call throughout the country went out for anything metal that could be spared. Americans scoured attics, garages, and kitchens for metal objects they could part with. New York City likes to do things with a flourish and to launch its drive, ten showgirls from the Broadway musical *Hellzapoppin'* raided the kitchen of the Algonquin Hotel for discarded cooking pots. Carrying them onto a fire truck, they banged away as the truck made its way to the Hotel Astor, where their kitchen raid was repeated. By the time New York City housewives depleted their kitchens, a huge mountain of pots, pans, percolators, and washboards rose at Times Square and another in front of City Hall.

That same month, while New York City was focusing on defending itself against German U-boats and flying bombers, President Roosevelt ordered all Japanese assets in the United States frozen, a response to Japan's occupation of Indochina. On August 1, a United States oil embargo was placed on all nations the president considered to be "aggressors." Japan was one of the bad fish caught in this net. During the spring and into the summer, articles would appear in the *New York Times* citing Japan's acts of hostility.

One of them involved four Japanese boat operators whose sampans had penetrated the heavily fortified channel leading to the U.S. naval base where the American fleet was anchored. Pearl Harbor's importance as a defense against attacks on America's coastline was not underestimated by the military. Notwithstanding those straying Japanese boatmen, however, the country's fear was an attack not by Japan but by the increasingly aggressive German air force. All eyes remained focused on the war in Europe.

November 26 was a sunny autumn Wednesday in New York. Women were shopping at Peck & Peck and at Best & Co. for their winter coats. Kids were lined up at the Criterion on Broadway and 45th Street to see Abbott & Costello in *Keep 'em Flying*, a slapstick comedy about the U.S. Air Corps. Edith Helen Backus walked down the aisle of St. Bartholomew's Church on Park Avenue with Jack Forker Chrysler, son of the man whose name is on one of the skyscrapers synonymous with the New York skyline. Theatergoers at the Martin Beck Theatre had caught a matinee of Lillian Hellman's *Watch on the Rhine*, a drama about an anti-Nazi agent who kills a Nazi sympathizer attempting to blackmail him. It was the latest of a dozen Broadway plays in the past few years whose themes expressed anti-Nazi sentiments. New Yorkers also learned that getting around town by taxi would soon cost them a nickel more for each fifth of a mile. In the early evening, as sports fans picked up their tickets at Madison Square Garden on Eighth Avenue and 50th Street for Friday night's fight between middleweight contenders Georgie Abrams and Tony Zale, Secretary of State Cordell Hull left his office in Washington, having concluded his meeting with the Japanese ambassador. Each promised further discussions between their two countries.

On that same day, in a harbor along the remote Kurile Islands north of Japan, thirty-three warships and six aircraft carriers had already slipped out of their berths and were headed east across the stormy North Pacific. On their decks were 420 bomber planes destined for Pearl Harbor.

PART II

WAR COMES TO NEW YORK CITY

So Far and Yet So Near

A VENDOR IN TIMES SQUARE distributes the *New York Enquirer*, announcing the attack on Pearl Harbor.

4

Where Were You When You Heard the News?

We were very, very frightened. We never thought there'd be another world war. Everybody around us was crying.

Bea Levine

Seven-year-old Don Israel was listening to the radio that Sunday afternoon. Nine-year-old Charles Rodin was at the Polo Grounds watching the football game between the Brooklyn Dodgers and the New York Giants. Joseph Dash, another nine-year old, was leaving the Kingsbridge Theater in the Bronx with his parents. They had just seen a Clark Gable movie. Eleven-year-old Tom McLaughlin was just coming out of a movie house on the Upper West Side. Fifteen-year-old Angela Lansbury, who was now an acting student, was passing a newsstand and stared at the headlines. Bill Vericker, who was seventeen, was playing football in Central Park.

Frances Kelly, the woman who would become his wife, was in a candy store on 188th Street. Nine-year-old Phillip Curtin was playing in his backyard in Woodside, Queens. Seventeen-year-old Martha Yamasaki was in her Japanese-American church on West 143rd Street. Ten-year-old Edna Satenstein was sitting at her desk polishing her nails. Her mother was knitting and her father was reading. David Lawrence, who was also ten, was with his parents, heading for a show at the Roxy. They had their car radio on. Mollie Heckerling was also in a car, driving back to the city from an outing with her brother and his friends. They, too, were listening to the radio.

Don Israel: "We had a wooden chest with a radio inside. I used to sit in front of it as a kid and listen to *The Green Hornet* and *The Shadow*. I remember sitting in front of it that Sunday when the announcer said that Pearl Harbor was bombed."

Bill Vericker: "We were leaving the park when we saw someone selling papers.

Newspapers printed on Saturday night. The only newspaper that printed on Sunday morning was the New York Enquirer. *That morning, they had a headline that read "Japs Attack Pearl Harbor." The newspaper boys were hawking it under the el. I remember my father looking at it and saying, "Boy, what some people will do to sell newspapers."*

—CHARLES RODIN

They had put out a quick extra edition. The newsboy was yelling 'Pearl Harbor Attacked!'"

Charles Rodin: "There actually was no announcement at the Polo Grounds. People who thought they remembered hearing it at the stadium were probably listening to it on the radio. I remember they kept paging Colonel William Donovan. He was head of the Office of Strategic Services."

Joseph Dash: "There was a candy store next to the theater. We saw people gathered around, riveted to the radio in the store. We went over to see what was going on and that's how we found out."

Tom McLaughlin: "As soon as I walked out of the theater I could see that something tremendous had happened. People's faces were ashen. I felt like running back into the theater. I remember later on, the frantic calls over the radio for all service personnel to report immediately to their duty stations."

Phillip Curtin: "My father looked out

the window and shouted, 'Pearl Harbor has been bombed!' It seemed as if an electric shock went through the whole neighborhood."

Edna Satenstein: "I didn't quite grasp it. Where was Pearl Harbor? My mother was so upset because her brother was there."

Angela Lansbury: "The front page of a newspaper was behind one of those wired boxes on the newsstand: 'Japanese Attack Pearl Harbor!' I'll never forget seeing that. Of course, as a British girl I was thrilled because America had finally come into the war."

David Lawrence: "We had the car radio on as we were entering the tunnel. You can't get any reception in the tunnel, but when we got out they were telling us in great staccato fashion that we were at war and that some unidentified planes had bombed Pearl Harbor. My father said, 'Well, we're in it.' I wasn't sure what that meant. People in line at the movie were all talking about it. Afterward we went to the Automat."

Martha Yamasaki: "I was in church. Japanese-American church services begin at two in the afternoon. At 2:30 a young man came racing up the steps shouting, 'Japan has bombed Pearl Harbor!' I was shocked. I never felt conscious of being a Japanese-American. I was an American reacting to this awful deed."

Mollie Heckerling: "We were horrified to hear that so many Americans were killed. We didn't yet realize the extent of what that would mean for the country."

Nineteen-year-old Bea Levine, married and the mother of a newborn girl, knew it was going to be bad: "We saw what was happening right before our eyes and we had to ask: What will happen? Where will this take us?"

New Yorkers who were tuned in to WOR's broadcast of the football game that the young Charles Rodin was attending were some of the first in the city to hear the news. It was December 7, 1941, 2:25 in the afternoon, with Brooklyn in possession of the ball on the 45-yard line, when an announcer's voice broke into the broadcast:

Japanese bombs have fallen on Hawaii and the Philippine Islands. Keep tuned to this station for further details. We now return you to the Polo Grounds.

Inside Radio City Music Hall, the audience was just beginning to watch Cary Grant charm Joan Fontaine in Alfred Hitchcock's *Suspicion* when the lights suddenly came on. Five-year-old Marilyn Tako was at the Music Hall and recalled her memories for the television documentary *75 Years at Radio City Music Hall*:

"A man came to the center of the stage and said: 'Pearl Harbor has been bombed by the Japanese. Everyone is to report to their units.' People were crying. I didn't know exactly what a war was or what was happening, but I knew that everyone was upset, so I was upset." Outside, people waiting on line to get into Radio City saw airplane-shaped pieces of paper drift down from the nearby offices of *Time* and *Life*. Before jettisoning them out the window, editors and writers had scrawled: "We are at war with Japan" on each of the paper airplanes. Listeners dialing up the Columbia Broadcasting System's broadcast of the New York Philharmonic, being carried on their New York outlet—then WABC—heard of the attack if they happened to tune in to John Charles Daly's newscast, which went on the air at 2:30, a half hour before the concert began:

> The Japanese have attacked Pearl Harbor Hawaii by air, President Roosevelt has just announced. The attack also was made on all military and naval activities on the principal island of Oahu.

Daly's stunning newscast went on for thirty-three minutes. When it was finished, the Philharmonic broadcast went on as usual, as did most scheduled programming in the city. Although Daly would repeat the news of the Japanese attack during the concert's intermission, the audience inside Carnegie Hall wasn't told what happened until the concert was over. As soon as the announcement was made, conductor Artur Rodzinki and Polish-born pianist Arthur Rubenstein, who had recently fled Paris after Hitler's invasion, performed a rousing "Star-Spangled Banner." Fritz Stern, who had escaped Nazi Germany with his parents, was at home listening: "I remember it was interrupted by the news bulletin. My parents were taking a nap and I had to wake them. I remember thinking, 'Am I the person who always brings the bad news to my parents?'"

New Yorkers got the news wherever they happened to be. Some who were out on the street hovered around car radios. For many it was simply word-of-mouth. Back then, most New Yorkers had never heard of Pearl Harbor. "Attacks on Pearl Harbor" was often misunderstood as "a tax on Pearl Harbor." By 4:00, thousands of people had gathered in Times Square, their eyes on the news zipper circling the *New York Times* Building as the ominous words *Japanese Air Raid on Honolulu* moved rapidly past their eyes.

Later that afternoon, inside the lounge of the Embassy Newsreel Theater on 50th Street just behind Radio City Music Hall, a television receiver was hastily set up on the stage. As a rapt audience sat and watched, NBC broadcast an awkwardly put-together impromptu news program. A reporter from *Collier's* magazine who was there grabbed a microphone and tried to provide some background on what led up to Japan's attack.

Mayor La Guardia was at home in his apartment on Fifth Avenue and 110th Street listening to the radio when the first bulletin came across. He raced out the door of his East Harlem building to the police radio car where John Peluso, his regular driver, was waiting for him. The car sped down Fifth Avenue, and within a short time it deposited the mayor in front of City Hall. Waiting for him inside were his Police, Fire, and Public Works commissioners. The three men followed the mayor into a conference room and when he emerged a short while later, New York City was on war alert. It was now the mayor's job, as he saw it, to prepare the city for the very real possibility that they were in the sights of the Japanese air force. "We are not out of the danger zone by any means," he warned New Yorkers in a hastily summoned press interview broadcast over WNYC, the city-owned station, at

5:15 that afternoon. The mayor barked into the microphone, ordering the citizens of his city to "toughen up" and be on the alert for "murder by surprise."

On orders from Washington, La Guardia had his police department place all Japanese nationals under house arrest. Within no time, squads of policemen fanned out into the city. They closed down the exclusive Nippon Club at 161 West 93rd Street, where wealthy, well-connected Japanese often socialized. They walked into the

AT 5:15 THAT SUNDAY AFTERNOON, Mayor La Guardia was being heard all over the city on WNYC radio.

Sukiyaki at 76 West 47th Street and the Miyako at 20 West 56th Street, two of the city's Japanese restaurants, and waited for diners to finish eating before escorting the owners and their staff to their homes. A guard was posted outside the Japanese Consulate in Rockefeller Center while inside the FBI went through their offices, impounding all records and documents. Guards arrived at the home of Japan's consul general, Morito Morishima, on East 70th Street and accompanied him back to the consulate office, where the stunned diplomat sequestered himself through the night. By Monday afternoon, after pleading the case for the detained Japanese nationals, Morishima would attempt to leave his office with a staff member who was carrying the consul general's briefcase. The two were intercepted. In Morishima's briefcase were twenty strips of film showing scenes of Washington, including the Washington Monument, shots of the New York skyline, and several bridges in both Washington and New York. There was also an image of what appeared to be a dam

or a reservoir. That Sunday, on orders from the State Department, all Japanese reservations out of New York's La Guardia Field and Idlewild Airport were canceled. Among the twenty Japanese nationals booked on Stratoliners were Morishima's wife and two children.

Within hours of the news of Japan's attack, the FBI had guards posted at the Croton and Kensico dams, at entrances to all of the city's tunnels and bridges, and at the Brooklyn Navy Yard, where two battleships, the *Missouri* and the *Iowa*, were under construction and where the newly commissioned *North Carolina*, considered to be a formidable sea weapon, was at anchor while her crew was in the city, enjoying liberty. Patrol boats were sent into the East River to make sure all vessels kept a distance from the shipyard. Guards were placed at steam plants and at telephone offices and radio broadcasting sites. All volunteer air-raid wardens and auxiliary Fire Department personnel were told they should report for daily drills until further

> *I was on the* Sante Fe Chief *bound for California. On the* Chief *one could rent a radio. You placed this little suction cup on the window and picked up the program. I called for a radio and was told, "There's no radio to be rented. Haven't you heard? The Japanese have just bombed Pearl Harbor. We're at war!"*
>
> —NORMAN CORWIN, WRITER, PRODUCER, *WE HOLD THESE TRUTHS*

notice. At about the time the mayor was racing down to City Hall, Rear Admiral Adolphus Andrews, commander of the North Atlantic Squadron, was en route to Manhattan from a dinner party on Long Island, the siren on his car blaring and the gas pedal close to the floor. By 3:45 Andrews was in his office at 90 Church Street, and within half an hour all prearranged plans for conditions of war were put into effect.

New York Harbor was placed on war footing as ships at anchor were searched for signs of sabotage. Leaves were canceled, and all officers and sailors were ordered to report for duty in full uniform by 8:00 the following morning. "We are not expecting any very large attack . . . ," Andrews told newsmen, adding, "Every possible step has been taken to protect the New York area from such an attack as surprised Pearl Harbor." Andrews did not believe Japanese planes could make it to the eastern seaboard. He was trying to reassure New Yorkers, unlike the fiery mayor, whose second broadcast that afternoon urged New Yorkers not to be lulled into a false sense of safety simply because the Japanese attack happened in the distant Pacific. "The situation is one of extreme crisis," warned the mayor, "with anything to be expected."

By evening, Grand Central Terminal and Pennsylvania Station were crowded with soldiers and sailors returning to their bases. Ethel Ursprung, a student at Hunter College, had taken a train to Grand Central Terminal that evening: "I never saw so many men in uniform. Everyone from men who had just signed up to officers in full uniform were there." On Grand Central's balcony Mary Lee Read, the house organist who often serenaded commuters, played the "Star-Spangled Banner." In Pennsylvania Station's main waiting room, a crowd gathered for the regularly scheduled Sunday evening concert given by the New York City Symphonic Band. As soon as Harwood Simmons lifted his baton, signaling the musicians to begin playing the national anthem, men's hats came off and women placed their right hands across their hearts. In White Plains, the America First Committee canceled their antiwar rally scheduled for Monday. Charles Lindbergh, who had sequestered himself on his Martha's Vineyard estate, would not speak with reporters. Later, he would join the former isolationist group in supporting President Roosevelt and offering his services to the nation.

That night, FBI agents went to the homes of Japanese aliens suspected of subversive activities. They were instructed to pack one suitcase, after which they were taken to nearby police stations where they were booked as "prisoners of the Federal authorities." Martha Yamasaki was visiting

JAPANESE, GERMAN,
and Italian aliens being rounded up on
December 9. They have just left a police wagon at the Battery and are about
to board a ferry that will take them to Ellis Island, where they are to be interned.

her uncle who worked for Mitsui, a Japanese exporter of fine fabric with offices in the Empire State Building. He was relaxing at home that Sunday evening when the doorbell rang. She recalled, "I opened the door to two well-dressed men who asked my uncle to accompany them. 'Just bring a toothbrush,' one of them said."

Among those arrested were Japanese newsmen assigned to Japan's powerful Mainichi newspapers, whose offices were just above those occupied by United Press. News correspondent Charles P. Arnot remembered that they were "frantic, effusively apologetic and just plain scared." Larry Tajiri, an American newspaperman of Japanese descent, was in Times Square that Sunday night with some colleagues with whom he worked at the *Pacific Citizen*. "We may have been a little ashamed of our faces as we walked through the crowded New York streets on that December night," he would later write. "We are American by every right, birth, education and belief, but our faces are those of the enemy . . ." The president of a Japanese bank who lived in a Park Avenue penthouse, was arrested, as was Keigi Hida, a silk importer whose address was the St. Moritz hotel. So was Dr. Sabro Emy, a graduate of New York University who had not been to Japan in seventeen years. The minister of the Methodist Church on 108th Street was arrested. Fujio Saito was there when he was taken away. He observes, "They were religious leaders, community leaders. I heard the minister remark as he was taken away, 'You don't know what freedom is until you're put into a camp.'" From the station house they were transported in squad cars to the Federal Building at Foley Square for further processing and then brought in small groups to the Barge office at the Battery. They were then put on ferries bound for Ellis Island, which was now shared with the U.S. Coast Guard as a training facility. Some were kept on Ellis Island for a few days or a few weeks and released. Those considered to be a threat to the security of America shared the same fate as Martha Yamasaki's uncle, who was eventually sent back to Japan on the SS *Gripsholm*. She reports, "We never saw him again."

Anger over the Japanese attack was swift and strong among New Yorkers and directed at anything Japanese. That afternoon, the Metropolitan Opera announced that it would not perform *Madame Butterfly* until Japan was defeated, even though the opera was composed by an Italian and sung in his language. (Ironically, on March 12, 1942, two FBI agents would show up at the home of Italian opera singer Ezio Pinza, who was suspected of being an enemy alien. Pinza was arrested and sent to Ellis Island, where he was interned for several months.) Within the next few days, the Japanese Pavilion at the World's Fair—a "monument to peace and goodwill" from the government of Japan—would be dismantled and the famous Japanese Garden in Brooklyn's Botanical Garden would be renamed the Oriental Garden. Another

> *It was a Sunday when we got the news. The next day, one of my classmates kept muttering, "Snakes in the grass! Snakes in the grass!"*
>
> —VIVIAN ROUSSO DULBERG

ROCKEFELLER CENTER'S BEAUTIFUL JAPANESE GARDEN, LOCATED on a setback on the eleventh floor, became a Chinese garden after Pearl Harbor.

Pearl Harbor, all Japanese-run enterprises including the handful of Japanese restaurants, all Japanese-run banks, silk stores, and art shops, and even the Japanese Methodist Church on West 143rd Street were ordered closed by the Federal Government until further notice. Yeichi "Kelly" Kuwayama's father had an import/export business on 47th Street, on the ground floor of the building where the Sukiyaki restaurant was located: "It ended with the bombing of Pearl Harbor. He moved what was left of his business into the Miyako." Although the restaurant was allowed to reopen, it would have few non-Asian customers during the war years. "Kelly," who was given the Irish nickname by his first sergeant because he couldn't pronounce Kuwayama, was already in the U.S. Army when Pearl Harbor was bombed, assigned to New York Harbor Defense. Once Pearl Harbor was attacked his artillery career ended, and the Princeton-educated American citizen became a purchasing clerk in an ordinance battalion away from New York

Japanese garden, one of the twelve that made up Rockefeller Center's "Gardens of the Nations" located on a setback on the eleventh floor of the RCA Building, was shorn of its chrysanthemums and replaced by a Chinese garden dedicated to Madame Chiang Kai-shek. Because of the recent trade restrictions with Japan there were fewer Japanese restaurants and stores in the city, but after the attack on

City. The boy who grew up in Woodside, Queens, amongst Italians, Czechs, and Germans would become part of an all-Japanese regiment, earning a silver star for his action in Italy, where, while badly wounded, he rescued a fellow soldier under enemy fire.

In White Plains, Matsusabo Matsushita, a fifty-year-old Japanese janitor who loved the Brooklyn Dodgers and spaghetti, was so ashamed of his native country he tried to commit hara-kiri. Teddy Hara was sent to Polyclinic Hospital after being beaten up in front of his rooming house on 46th Street and Ninth Avenue. Not surprisingly, Walter Winchell got into the act that night as he delivered his broadcast over the airwaves: *"Persons who arouse suspicions by their conduct, speech, or deed are inviting microscopic examination, perhaps prison,"* he shouted in his familiar staccato delivery. *"Nothing matters any more now except national security."*

By dawn the next morning, while Japanese prisoners awaited their fate on Ellis Island, Army fighting planes were taking off from Mitchel Field on Long Island, joining an airborne Navy patrol in an effort to guard the city from potential air attacks. Anti-aircraft observation posts were put into position all over the city, including Brooklyn's Prospect Park and Manhattan's Bryant Park.

ARTIST MEYERS ROHOWSKY'S depiction of the anti–air-raid observation post installed in Bryant Park shortly after Pearl Harbor. In the background is the New York Public Library.

It had to be an unsettling sight for New Yorkers leaving their office buildings in the early evening to suddenly see huge searchlights behind the New York Public Library scanning the skies for enemy aircraft while nearby, gun-toting military guards protected them. The mayor's volunteer air-raid wardens had been on duty since midnight, as had the airplane spotters, perched on roofs in all five boroughs. Teachers in all of the city's eight hundred schools were instructed to get their pupils

IF MEN COULDN'T MAKE IT TO THE ENLISTMENT center, the U.S. Navy brought the enlistment center to them. This is the Navy's first recruitment bus, parked in Washington Square.

home as soon as they heard an air-raid alarm.

American flags were everywhere, hung from every window and lining every avenue. Before the war, Fifth Avenue had become a battleground between isolationists and those who wanted to come to the aid of our Allies. Each group would stake out one side of the avenue and lure people with their posters and pamphlets. Now, all of Fifth Avenue was awash in red, white, and blue. By early morning, long lines had formed around all of the city's Army, Navy, and Marine recruitment centers. As Japanese nationals continued to arrive in the Federal Court House for processing,

A SERVICEMAN AND BARTENDER AT THE STORK Club listen as President Roosevelt delivers his "A Date Which Will Live in Infamy" speech, broadcast at noon on Monday, December 8.

just a few blocks away more than a thousand men who had come to 90 Church Street to sign up for the Navy had to be turned away because the line for processing had already grown too long.

At noon that Monday, all of New York City came to a standstill to listen to President Roosevelt's address to the nation. In City Hall Park, where over five thousand people had gathered, loudspeakers were mounted on a WNYC sound truck. Courts adjourned shortly before noon so that judges, lawyers, and jury members could listen to the president's speech. Inside the stock exchange it grew so quiet, a clerk could close his eyes and believe he was in a pew in nearby Trinity Church. Anywhere there was a radio there was a crowd. People gathered around newsstands, in bars, and around cars and taxis that had come to a halt. In Times Square, they gathered in clusters to listen to any available radio. Men who were outdoors silently removed their hats as the "Star-Spangled Banner" was played. If a sense of determination hadn't already gripped New Yorkers, President Roosevelt's now-famous "A Date Which Will Live in Infamy" speech was the glue that gave the city its unified voice. Joan Harris was ten years old when war broke out. She recalls, "All of us were grouped around the radio. The older people were very, very shook up and worried."

In the days that followed, Mayor La Guardia, as head of the Office of Civil Defense, began to implement his plan to prepare New York City for the Japanese attack that he knew would occur. In his fiery speeches, he would always say "when" an attack comes, and never "if." On Tuesday, December 9, it appeared that his warnings were not mere hysteria. As air-raid wardens and airplane spotters were getting ready to report for duty, a bulletin from the Associated Press made banner headlines in the evening edition of the *Baltimore News-Post*:

N.Y. WARNED ENEMY PLANES
ARE NEAR CITY.

> *I showed up . . . in a blue suit and a skinny orange tie, ready to meet my fate along with hundreds of other eligible teenagers. In the massive induction center you could see a city block of faces: sad and cocky, confused, and some terror-stricken by the whole process.*
>
> —COMEDIAN JERRY LEWIS, TWO DAYS BEFORE HIS EIGHTEENTH BIRTHDAY

Rumors had spread that at Long Island's Mitchel Field, where the First Air Force was stationed, unidentified planes had been spotted off the East Coast and were just two hours away from New York City. The planes turned out to belong to the U.S. Navy, but had Japanese aircraft been in sight of the Empire State Building, the citizens of New York City at whom the mayor had been screaming would have been in for a terrible surprise.

That morning, the mayor had ordered a borough-wide "alert" to test the city's air-raid system. He got to witness not only the confusing inadequacy of the system, but the typical New Yorker's exasperating indifference to

it. The citizens of his city would line up day after day at recruitment centers, trying to get themselves into the armed forces, and would show up wherever needed to volunteer their time and talents, but unless they could see the Japanese flag painted on the belly of an aircraft, they were not likely to take air-raid drills too seriously.

ITALIAN-AMERICAN women stand on their fire escapes and cheer a parade on Mott Street honoring boys from the neighborhood who have joined the Army.

THE WEATHER
Clear and somewhat colder tonight
with the lowest temperature around
25 degrees. Wednesday, increasing
cloudiness and moderately cold.

Detailed Weather Report on Page 36

MEAN TEMPERATURES YESTERDAY

Baltimore	42	New York	35
Atlanta	46	Omaha	37
Boston	32	Portland, Maine	22
Chicago	33	Salt Lake City	34
Jacksonville	53	San Antonio	54
Los Angeles	63	Seattle	43
Miami	74	Tampa	62
New Orleans	52	Washington	42

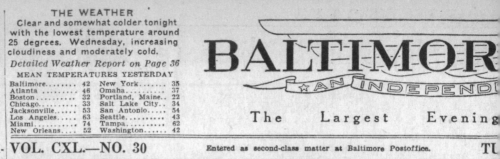

BALTIMOR

☆ AN INDEPEND

The Largest Evening

VOL. CXL.—NO. 30

Entered as second-class matter at Baltimore Postoffice.

TU

MR. CHARLES S. RYCKMAN has contributed
to this column today a
wonderful article urging the
regular and continued observance of Bible Week in America.

Nothing could be more important than this observance
to our country and our people
in these troublous times, when
the nation seems to be altering not only its historic political institutions but its characteristic standards of faith
and worship.

A return to basic religion,
to inspirational truth — to
genuine democracy and to elemental honesty and sincerity
—is what America seems to
need and what loyal Americans desire.

How can that renaissance of
reverence for all that is uplifting and ennobling better be
secured than by careful and
constant reading of the main
source of our moral and religious teachings—the Bible?

Even as King David sang:

*"Thy Word is a lamp unto
my feet, and a light unto my
path."*

And as Whittier wrote:

*"We search the world for
truth; we cull
The good, the pure, the beautiful
From graven stone and written scroll,
From all old flower fields of
the soul;
And, weary seekers of the
best,
We come back laden from our*

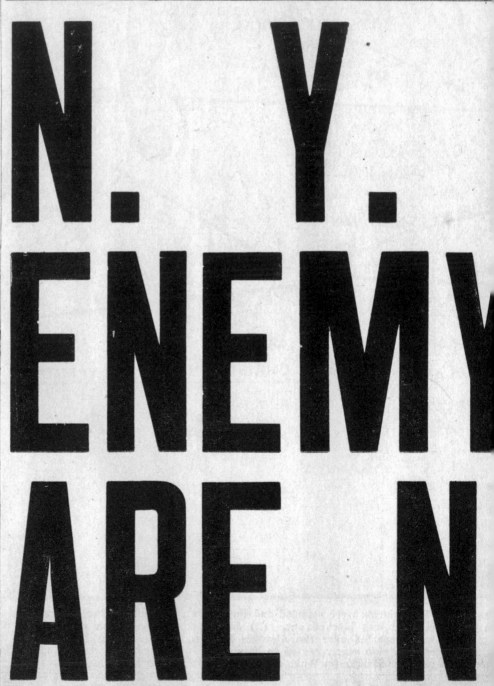

N. Y.
ENEMY
ARE N

THE NEWS-POST

NEWSPAPER

...rculation in the Entire South

EVENING, DECEMBER 9, 1941   PRICE **3** CENTS

7

HOME FINAL

WARNED PLANES ...AR CITY

The sirens were pretty pathetic. Until a better system was put in place, the city had to rely on police car sirens and the more powerful ones on fire trucks. But all the mayor could think of were those kamikaze pilots aiming their planes' noses at his city as New Yorkers behaved like New Yorkers. Along Fifth Avenue, Christmas shoppers were too busy sprinting from Bonwit Teller's to Best & Co. to pay attention to a screaming air-raid warden. In Times Square, as air wardens donned asbestos gloves while perched atop the roof of the Paramount Building, ready to snuff out incendi-

ITALIAN-AMERICAN WOMEN PARTICIPATE IN A flag-raising ceremony. The Italian-American community wanted their neighbors to know that their loyalty was with America and not Mussolini.

ary bombs with their shovels and carts heaped with sand, people below milled around the Times Tower checking the electronic zipper for the latest war news. Passengers on downtown buses stared indifferently at policemen who were barking at them to get off the buses and find shelter. Inside movie houses, films played without interruption. An exasperated Captain John J. E. Appel, commander of the West 54th Street police station, threw up his hands in the face of the Broadway theater district's indifference to the alarms, at the same time letting people know that these drills should be handled as if they were "a blackout and not a carnival affair." The other boroughs didn't behave much better. "Bewildered," "indifferent," and "nonchalant" were the

ITALIAN SEAMEN LEAVE ELLIS ISLAND EN route to a detention camp in Montana. Note one man giving the fascist salute.

adjectives borough officials used to describe their citizenry.

Those adjectives vanished on December 11 when Germany and Italy declared war on the United States. Suddenly, a quiet resolve swept over the city. Reporters interviewing New Yorkers in Yorkville, on the Upper West Side and the Lower East Side, in Harlem, Park Slope, Flushing, Washington Heights, and on Staten Island's Todt Hill found that all were of the same mind: there was a war to be won, and the time had come to roll up our sleeves and start winning it. At a meeting at National House, 150 Japanese-Americans condemned Japan's attack on Pearl Harbor, as well as its invasion of China and French Indochina. Italian-Americans picking up their copy of *Il Progresso* would read an editorial by Generoso Pope, the paper's formerly pro-Mussolini editor, strongly instructing his six million readers to pledge unconditional loyalty to the United States. Young Italian-Americans were quick to line up at enlistment centers. Their parents and grandparents lowered their heads and whispered *"vergonia,"* the Italian word for "shame" and "dishonor," as images of the Italian dictator were hastily removed from store windows and replaced by those of President Roosevelt. In predominantly Jewish Bensonhurst, Italian-born Carolina Madeo would sit on her stoop with the *Daily News* or the *Daily Mirror.* Invariably one of the tabloids would have a photo of Mussolini or Hitler on the front page. Making sure her non-Italian neighbors saw her, the woman whose four sons enlisted in the service would throw the newspaper onto the sidewalk and grind her heel into the face of the enemy, swearing at it in her native Italian.

Yorkville was particularly tense, temporarily closing its movie houses lest people think they were showing German movies. At Rockefeller Center, the entrance to the Palazzo D'Italia was deprived of its coat of arms, and Italian sculptor Attilio Piccirilli's cartouche depicting commerce and industry above the entrance to 636 Fifth Avenue was covered with wooden planks. The handsome work of art had the misfortune of being cast in 1936, when Mussolini came into power. German and Italian tenants now followed the Japanese, who had already been evicted from the complex. Once more, the FBI ordered the arrest of suspicious aliens and by Thursday, December 11, 165 Germans and 65 Italians joined the 241 Japanese being held on Ellis Island. In all of this there was also vindication for Mayor La Guardia, who had been accused of being Chicken Little, unduly frightening New Yorkers with his feisty words of warning.

Now, New Yorkers took every air-raid drill seriously. Times Square was considered a major target. At the Hotel Astor, 750 air-raid wardens were called to a meeting where a plan was quickly implemented to place the area stretching from 42nd to 50th Street on

> *We shipped out on the* Queen Elizabeth. *When I got on the ship I could see 44th Street. If I screamed loud enough I could have let my family know I was here. I grew up in this neighborhood!*
>
> —BILL SHAW

THIS PHOTO-MURAL, measuring seventy-five feet high and thirty feet wide and promoting the sale of defense bonds, hung above the servicemen's lounge in Grand Central Terminal.

a complete war footing. "Lights Out!" could have been the code as Local 3 of the International Brotherhood of Electrical Workers and the Theatrical Protective Union pledged to put together a grand synchronization to douse all of the Great White Way's lights at the first sound of an alert. Theater managers agreed to stop plays and turn off lights as soon as they got the signal. To test the system, thirty-second mini-blackouts were conducted on all four East River bridges and on the Empire State Building. At 9:00 on December 13, a Friday evening, all of the lights on

45th Street between Sixth and Ninth avenues in the heart of the theater district were briefly turned off. Audiences watching *Lady in the Dark* were literally without lights.

As large office buildings began to hang blackout shades and cover other windows with black paint, a meeting was held in the State Office Building at 80 Centre Street. The topic was the possible evacuation of women and children should the city come under attack. Suddenly, New Yorkers were being referred to as "refugees" as plans for a mass evacuation were being seriously discussed.

Meanwhile, New York looked the part of a city at war. In Grand Central Terminal a huge photo mural that reached to the ceiling was hung at the east end of the main concourse, taking up the entire wall. The mural was installed to kick off a bond drive, but as sol-

THIS AIR-RAID TEST siren was being placed on top of a truck at the corner of Spring and Lafayette streets before its permanent installation atop one of the city skyscrapers. The five-horsepower siren was designed to be heard within a radius of three to five miles.

80

diers on Christmas furloughs arrived here from their training camps for a few nights on the town, the montage of battleships, airplanes, tanks, and a war plant couldn't help but remind them of what lay ahead. Downtown in City Hall, Mayor La Guardia converted the city's seat of government into a kind of "war central." "Preservationists be damned!" he might as well have said when he gave the go-ahead for large holes to be bored into the historic building's marble floors. The holes were for the iron fences the mayor was having installed to barricade his office from the large volunteer civilian defense staff who would be working in the building. The "war zone" look was complete when makeshift offices and a defense information center were erected around the rotunda circling the building's Italian Renaissance staircase.

From his desk on Sunday evening, a week after the attack on Pearl Harbor, the mayor delivered one of his radio chats, never softening his ominous message: "We have never had war by a foreign enemy brought to the streets of our city and right into our homes. The truth is that we are in serious danger . . . if our enemies have an opportunity to bomb our city they will do so." The next day, five air-raid sirens—the first of seventy—were delivered to the city. The "big whistle," with its three-to-five-mile range, was already mounted on the edifice of the New

York Edison Company at 40th Street and the East River. The mayor was also requisitioning gas masks—fifty million of them—including a "Mickey Mouse" version for little children. Fearing that an initial wave of air attacks on the city would be aimed at its vital piers, the city's fire commissioner ordered five hundred longshoremen to show up in front of the Grace Line at the foot of 15th Street, where they were taught how to be vigilant and watch for anything that might ignite the buildings, all of which contained highly combustible materials. There was even talk of barring visitors from seeing off passengers on departing ships. To prevent saboteurs from planting bombs, public lockers were sealed off in subways, in Pennsylvania Station and Grand Central Terminal, and in bus terminals and ferry waiting rooms.

By mid-December, ads appeared in New York newspapers selling makeshift air-raid shelter kits that could be erected in backyards. Abercrombie & Fitch was selling steamship chairs, rugs, and foot warmers, advertising them as "the perfect Christmas presents for the airplane spotter in your family." In an effort to promote safety over vanity, handbags at Lord & Taylor replaced compacts with flashlights and mini first-aid kits. Several Woolworth stores around town had separate "Blackout Necessities" counters with bandages and flashlights, and Macy's had

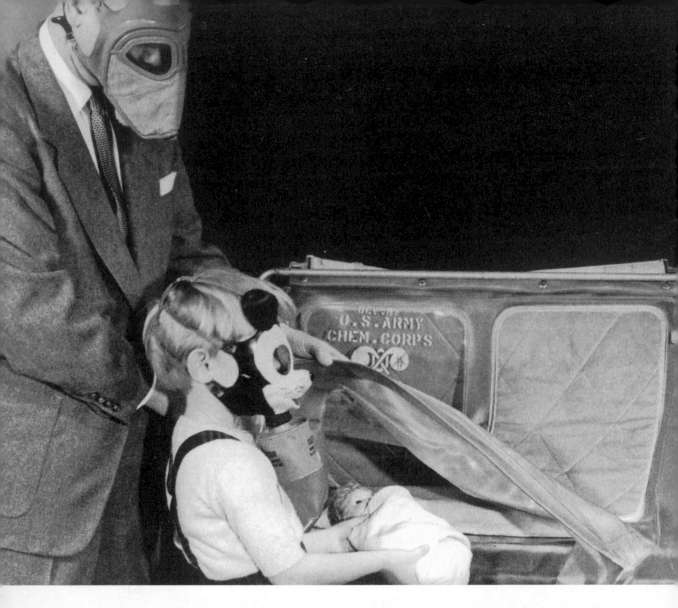

ONE MONTH AFTER PEARL HARBOR, the Sun Rubber Company introduced this Mickey Mouse gas mask for children. The cartoon design was meant to diminish fear by getting the children to wear the masks as a game.

its own Blackout Nook—appropriately in its basement—where it sold sandhog helmets that had been modified for air-raid use.

On Christmas Eve over a thousand men and women reported to their local precincts to sign up as air-raid wardens, and on Christmas Day half that number left their turkey dinners to enroll. They joined the more than two thousand New

Yorkers who already wore the now familiar red and white armband. The following day Boy Scouts fanned out through the five boroughs, distributing 18,000 air-raid posters. And on the night before New Year's Eve, residents of Far Rockaway in Queens looked up at the night sky and watched a mock air attack as six enormous searchlights aimed their beams on U.S. Army airplanes.

As the eyes of New Yorkers were fixed on the skies, watching mock air attacks or following the beams from the two giant Sperry searchlights in Bryant and Prospect parks, another kind of danger was about to get their attention. On December 10, just three days after Germany declared war on the United States, Admiral Karl Doenitz, the brilliant officer who headed Germany's submarine fleet, was informed that U.S. ships in the Atlantic were no longer off-limits to the German navy's torpedoes. This was the news Doenitz had been waiting for. Japan had just badly crippled the U.S. naval fleet and the country's vital eastern shore was defenseless. Doenitz eyed it all, including New York's famous harbor. Now was the time to strike, and what better weapon than the one that sent so many of Britain's ships to the bottom of the sea? The U-boats were coming. And the waters around New York City were in their sights.

THE ROCKEFELLER CENTER CHORISTERS serenading New Yorkers with Christmas concerts. Four live reindeer flanked the traditional Norway spruce at Rockefeller Center in 1941. Throughout the war years, the sight of the tree at Christmas brought comfort to New Yorkers.

U-Boats at Our Shores!

Some people told us that the other night they saw a freighter on the horizon get hit. From the beach they could hear the explosion and see the flames.

Richard McDermott
Sea Bright, New Jersey

In the third week of December 1941, as New Yorkers Christmas-shopped along Fifth Avenue, stopping to see the eighty-three-foot Norwegian spruce tree lit with eight hundred red and blue bulbs in Rockefeller Center's sunken plaza, the first of five German U-boats left its submarine pen at Lorient on France's Bay of Biscay and headed for New York City. The other four, destined for different points along America's eastern seaboard, were not far behind. Admiral Doenitz, Hitler's naval commander, had a brilliant plan. Doenitz envisioned a simultaneous attack up and down the eastern coast of the United States, one whose psychological impact could be as devastating as the lethal damage it would inflict. Japan's attack on the U.S. naval fleet in Hawaii had surprised Germany as much as it did the United States, and now the man in charge of Germany's U-boats saw an opportunity to strike at America when she was most vulnerable.

In his fifteenth-floor office at 90 Church Street, Admiral Andrews—"Dolly" to his colleagues—knew what was coming. British intelligence got wind of Doenitz's plans early on and by Christmas Eve, as Winston Churchill was arriving at the White House to discuss war strategy, President Roosevelt knew everything about the planned attack except when it would occur. Andrews's job was to guard the coastline from North Carolina to Canada—fifteen hundred miles of it—with ships and aircraft. There was one major problem: the admiral had at his immediate disposal only twenty ships, the largest of which was a 165-foot Coast Guard cutter, and about one hundred aging airplanes. Those ships, according to Edwin P. Hoyt, " . . . could all be anchored in New York's 79th Street yacht basin on the Hudson River with room to spare." The planes at La Guardia Air Field wouldn't be of much use. On December 10, an underwater anti-submarine net was strung two miles below the Narrows, from Norton's Point on the western

edge of Coney Island to Hoffman Island, a merchant marine training center off Staten Island, in hopes of preventing the U-boats from entering the harbor. Andrews wanted to place mines even closer to the shoreline, but he couldn't chance having large vessels attempt to make their way safely through the mine fields unless they were escorted by patrol boats with knowledge of where those mines were placed. And he had no patrol boats. All he could do was sit and wait.

On January 13, a number of submarines had been sighted three hundred miles off the coast of Nantucket moving south toward New York. At 1:20 the following morning, the tanker *Norness* was sixty miles southeast of Montauk Point, traveling out to sea, when a violent explosion rocked her side. Suddenly a shower of fuel oil was cascading over her deck. The captain thought the ship had hit one of the mines placed there by the Navy a month before, but in the dark, oil-slicked water, as he and his crew were making their escape in a motorboat, they could hear "guttural voices" coming from what appeared to be a surfaced submarine. After two more torpedoes were fired into her, the *Norness* disappeared into the Atlantic. Germany's U-boat attack on America had begun.

Doenitz gave this first onslaught of America's coastline a code name: he called it Operation *Paukenschlag* or Drumbeat, picturing his deadly U-boats having the same numbing effect as the constant pounding on a drum. The U-boat that sank the *Norness* had only just begun its deadly mission. Reinhard Hardegen, its twenty-eight-year-old commander, had instructions to proceed to Ambrose Lightship at the entrance to Lower New York Bay, where he would wait for fuel-laden tankers and freighters leaving New York Harbor. Once it had done its damage there, Hardegen's submarine would proceed south to Cape Hatteras for more targets.

In what remained of the predawn hours, the U-boat made its way toward New York City, hugging the south shore of Long Island and using the street lamps and lights from an occasional early-rising household as beacons. With the rising sun, the U-boat was forced to descend to the ocean's floor, where it awaited the darkness. It was a Wednesday morning, a weekday like any other. As New Yorkers were getting out of bed and going to work or bringing their children to school, they couldn't know that just off Long Beach, on the Rockaway peninsula, a group of young German sailors sealed in their submarine at the bottom of the ocean were sitting down to breakfast. As listeners tuned in their radios at 8:45 that morning, some would be flipping the dial to

WOR for *The Goldbergs*, a popular comedy show about a working-class Jewish family in New York City, at the same moment when one of the baffled U-boat crew members was doing the same, wondering what he was listening to.

The night was clear and cold when the U-boat resurfaced. One of the U-boat crew members saw a bright beam of light in the distance. Thinking it was the Ambrose Lightship, he steered the submarine toward it, not realizing that the beam was coming from land and that if they followed it for a few more minutes, they would find themselves grounded on Rockaway beach. Like the Lorelei, the beautiful Rhine maidens who lured sailors to their doom, the lure of the lightship had nearly been their demise. In a further note of irony, the submarine crew would never locate the Ambrose Lightship because it had been temporarily moved to Cape Cod.

The U-boat continued toward New York Harbor, past the carnival lights of Coney Island's Wonder Wheel and the Parachute Jump, keeping clear of land as it neared Lower New York Bay. Commander Hardegen expected to see Navy warships in the area. He assumed the U.S. Navy had peppered the waters with mines. Still he pressed on, urged by the need to reach New York City. It was 10:00 when the U-boat approached the area south of where the lightship usually anchored. The tip of Manhattan lay just beyond the Narrows. The temptation to keep going when he was so close must have at moments been irresistible to the young Hardegen, who would later write about what he felt that night: "I cannot describe the feeling with words, but it was unbelievably beautiful and great. I would have given away a kingdom for this moment if I had one. We were the first to be here, and for the first time in this war a German soldier looked out upon the coast of the U.S.A." For Hardegen, that moment was not about conquest but about seeing the glow from this dazzling, incandescent city—one he had visited once before as a young boy. Hardegen "wondered what form the life of the city was taking at that hour . . . Were the Broadway shows just letting out? Were the jazz clubs just getting started? Were the newsboys hawking the last editions—or the first?" In his imagination he fantasized how clever it would be to walk around Times Square and tip his cap to passers-by.

Although hungry to find another target, Hardegen was beginning to feel like a sitting duck. Surely, the U.S. Navy had anticipated the possibility of some uninvited guests. Where were the large ships that usually trafficked the city's harbor? Was this a trap waiting to snap itself shut on him? When no large vessels appeared

on the horizon, Hardegen headed back out to sea. He was just off Quogue, a summer waterfront community on Long Island's South Shore, when he got his wish. In his sites was the *Coimbra,* a British tanker capable of delivering eighty thousand barrels of oil to fuel-starved England. With one torpedo, the oil-laden ship erupted into a massive ball of flames. The fire was so intense that Long Islanders could see its deathly glow from their homes. Several of them notified the Coast Guard. All they would be able to do was clean up the debris. The captain, along with his thirty-five man crew, perished.

It was just the beginning. With the torpedoing of the Norwegian tanker *Varanger* on January 25, just thirty-five miles off the resort town of Sea Isle, New Jersey, Germany's U-boats had sunk six Allied ships—six ships filled with precious cargo (not to mention the lives lost) sent to the bottom of the sea in less than two weeks. By the end of January the figure would soar to thirteen. Andrews's hands were tied. Washington was of no help; no one there had a clue about

GERMAN SPIES HAD BEEN INFILTRATING THE UNITED States since the 1930s, but now that German U-boats were operating just off New York and New Jersey's shores, it became imperative that Americans understand their potential danger.

fighting submarines. Winston Churchill suggested using convoys to protect the Liberty ships that had been built expressly to carry cargo during the war. But in this first full month of the war, there were no convoys to be had. It was treacherous for any ship traveling beyond the 100-fathom curve where the continental shelf drops into deep water. This was where the U-boats would hide during daylight.

There was something else that was putting the ships in grave harm: if they traveled the waters up and down the Atlantic coast at night, their silhouettes were illuminated by the lights of the towns they passed. They became easy targets, waiting to be picked off by the unseen U-boats. Andrews wanted the lights dimmed, but since a directive would have to be issued from Washington, all he could do was suggest this. And in this early stage of the war, even as gobs of oil washed up onto New Jersey's famous beaches, local businessmen were reluctant to go along with him. Atlantic City was enjoying a lively winter season, with its five golf courses booked and its boardwalk crowded with strollers and bicyclists. For the busy resort town, dim-outs would be bad for business.

The months ahead would prove the costliness of this decision. At 7:00 on a cold February evening, the American tanker *India Arrow*, en route to New York City from Corpus Christi, Texas, with a full load of fuel, went down in a spectacular blaze off Atlantic City along with most of her crew. Residents of nearby Sea Isle heard their windows rattle as the ship exploded. Those who were near the beach watched in amazement as ribbons of burning oil turned the horizon a bright red. On February 28, the U.S. destroyer *Jacob Jones* left the Brooklyn Navy Yard to search for survivors of a ship that had been torpedoed earlier, only to be hit as well. Sleepy Jersey shore residents were awakened by the ghastly inferno that sent most of the ship's crew to their deaths.

By March, the U-boats had gotten even more aggressive. Beach walkers along the New Jersey and Long Island shores would come upon oil-soaked life preservers, chunks of charred rope, and tins of food rations. The occasional huge burning flash on the horizon meant another ship had been torpedoed. Richard McDermott was celebrating his eleventh birthday with his aunt and uncle whose house in Sea Bright, New Jersey, was a block away from the shore. "There was debris on the beach and we were told by the guys who were patrolling it that it came from torpedoed ships," he recalls. The encounters with U-boats were also becoming more visible. On March 14 as vacationers were out for a stroll on Atlantic City's boardwalk, two tankers not far from shore were traveling north with a German U-boat in hot pursuit. As spectators watched, one of the tankers took a torpedo, burned, and disappeared. A few days later in that same spot, another U-boat was chasing a tanker. They were both so close to shore that when the torpedo missed the ship it kept on going until it slammed onto the beach, where it promptly exploded. U-boats were now becoming so brazen that they no longer submerged after an attack.

By April, confident that the U.S. Navy was incapable of thwarting them, U-boats were attacking in broad daylight. Now, along with the life preservers and flame-singed debris from sunken ships, bodies were washing up on shore. The situation was desperate. By the end of March, President Roosevelt took back seventy aircraft that had been built for the British and ordered them delivered to the U.S. Navy. Blimps that could hover over the ocean and supposedly spot submarines were also being built. But none of them were here yet, and Admiral Andrews was in a panic.

Help would soon arrive from a group of millionaire yachtsmen. In February 1942, when it was obvious to any New Yorker who read a newspaper that the Navy was doing precious little to stem the devastating U-boat attacks just off their shore, the Cruising Club of America came knocking at its door, offering to place a small flotilla of good-sized sailing yachts along with their experienced crews at its disposal. Commander Vincent Astor volunteered to run the show and among the yachts lent to the Navy were those belonging to Henry Ford, Huntington Hartford, and the DuPont family, as well as William K. Vanderbilt's $3 million *Alva.* In June, these barons of commerce became part of the Coastal Picket Patrol, their mahogany-clad yachts armed with machine guns as they prepared to sail around

> *We lived in Bradley Beach, New Jersey, south of Asbury Park. My father was an air-raid warden and he patrolled the boardwalk. He would tell us about seeing the gun flashes when it was pitch black way out on the ocean. We'd go down to the beach some mornings and I remember seeing the oil slick, the wood, and cans of Planter's Peanuts.*
>
> —DON ISRAEL

THE MORTALLY WOUNDED *NORMANDIE* could be seen through banks of smoke by visitors on Rockefeller Center's Observation Roof. It was from this vantage point that NBC televised the disaster and photographers took shots of the listing ship.

New York Harbor on the lookout for U-boats. They were soon joined by volunteer pilots with their own Cessnas and Luscombes. Fitted with depth charges and demolition bombs, the colorful little planes—painted bright red, blue, and yellow—became a familiar sight to people along the shore as they hovered over shipping lanes in the daylight hours, hoping to prevent the audacious U-boats from surfacing.

Then, on June 18, rumors began to circulate that enemy agents were sitting in hotel rooms along Asbury Park and Atlantic City, flashing signals to nearby submarines. There was also talk that members of submarine crews were swimming ashore at night and meeting up with other agents. This was not surprising. German spies had been operating in this country with very little censure since the 1930s, taking jobs in factories and in bars along the Manhattan, New Jersey, and Brooklyn waterfront. As bartenders they could very easily pick up vital information from seamen. Some had worked on American ships during peacetime, placing them above suspicion. In *The American Home Front: 1941–1942*, Alistair Cooke tells the story of an American seaman whose tanker was torpedoed by a U-boat. In perfect English, the submarine commander asked if anyone was hurt. One of the men suffered a badly mangled leg and after bringing him on the submarine, where his wounds were patched up, the submarine commander asked whether any of the crew were from Brooklyn. He then boasted in perfect Brooklynese, "Maybe I worked with some o' you guys. I was twelve years in the Brooklyn Navy Yard."

The undermining fear of sabotage and its consequences visited New York City on a cold, clear Monday in February. It was shortly after 2:30 on the afternoon of the ninth. Over at Pier 88 on West 49th Street, Clement Derrick was removing the last of four stanchions in the Grand Salon of the SS *Normandie*, which was in the process of being converted to the troopship

SS *Lafayette*. As his welder's torch penetrated the metal, sparks suddenly spat out onto nearby bales of burlap that had been wrapped around the ship's highly flammable life preservers. The resulting shower of fire could not be quenched, and by 3:00 much of the luxury liner, the pride of a once-free France, was engulfed in flames. Plumes of black smoke were reaching across Manhattan, propelled by a brisk northwest wind. New Yorkers looked up as the oily smoke became a scrim across the midday sun. Mayor La Guardia was in the middle of a radio speech assuring New Yorkers that the nickel subway fare would not be raised when word of the burning *Normandie* reached him. The mayor quickly cut short his speech and raced to the pier. By now hundreds of New Yorkers, following the smoke and the sounds of sirens, had arrived to watch as streams of water from a line of fireboats tried in vain to stop the blaze. Bellevue Hospital sounded its dreaded seven bells—the signal for a city-wide catastrophe—and at nearby Pier 92 where the *Queen Mary* and *Queen Elizabeth* had their berths, a makeshift hospital was set up for the workers who were being carried off the stricken ship. Isabelle Sefton was a young woman when the *Normandie* caught fire. She recalls, "My father was a doctor at St. Clare's Hospital on 50th and Ninth Avenue. When word of the *Normandie* burning reached the hospital, he was one of a contingent of doctors who went over there to see what they could do." Tom McLaughlin could see the smoke from his window on Riverside Drive and 122nd Street. In Brooklyn, Alan Walden's father said to him, "Something has happened on the Hudson River." The pair boarded a subway to Manhattan and made their way to the pier. The young Walden remembered "seeing this immense cloud of smoke coming out of this huge gray ship which was tilting in the water." Crowds of people had gathered for blocks along the waterfront. As the fire continued to rage, more fireboats arrived. For hours their fountains of water kept flooding the ship's cabins. Soon there was more water than fire. Then, at 3:40 in the afternoon, just as the mayor, accompanied by Admiral Andrews, was attempting to board the wounded vessel, she suddenly lurched several feet to port. This was the beginning of the end.

The deathwatch took on a carnival atmosphere as skyscraper windows all over the city were thrown open so New Yorkers could watch the awful spectacle. The pier was alive with firemen and ambulance crews, with hawkers and food vendors to feed them, all watching as the great ship began to drown from the firewater that was meant to save her. It took twelve hours for the *Normandie* to die. At precisely 2:35 the following morning, with the acrid smell of burning metal still hanging over Times Square, the elegant creature rolled over on her port side and gave up her fight. The following day, thousands of New Yorkers showed up at the pier to gape at the destroyed ship. Five-year-old Miki Rosen saw it from the inside of the family car: "My father wanted us to see it because it was an historical event. I was terribly frightened by this enormous thing that I knew was supposed to be upright and bobbing up and down. It didn't even look like a ship. It was a mass of iron floating in the water."

Talk of sabotage was in the air. Had someone slit the fire hoses? Were German spies working on the ship? Was it perhaps gasoline that spurted from the sprinkler system? Ironically, in Alfred Hitchcock's spy thriller *Saboteur*, released just two months after the ship was destroyed, a German agent by the name of Frank Fry fills the fire extinguishers in a California airplane plant with gasoline, igniting a catastrophic fire. Hitchcock was in post-production of the film when the *Normandie* caught fire. Seizing an opportunity to sharpen the plot, he obtained a newsreel of the ship and had Norman Lloyd, who played the German agent, ride in a taxi up the West Side Highway. As he passes the stricken ship, Lloyd looks out the window and smiles smugly, indicating to the au-

NEW YORKERS WERE DRAWN TO THE SIGHT of the *Normandie* on its side in the Hudson River. On a deeper level, the crowds that gathered daily to witness the disaster felt vulnerable. "Was it sabotage?" they wondered as they stared at the burned-out hulk.

dience that one more act of sabotage has been successful.

For New Yorkers and the entire country, the possibility that the once glorious ship was brought down by Germany or the Vichy government was very real. In September 1941, thirty-three German agents were put on trial in a Brooklyn court-room, led there by counterespionage agent William Sebold, a thirty-three-year-old German-American. Operating under the name "Harry Sawyer," Sebold was set up in an office on 42nd Street where the FBI observed his meetings with New York-based spies through a two-way mirror. A year before Sebold was put on the case,

MADE BEFORE AMERICA'S ENTRY INTO THE WAR, WARNER
Bros.' 1939 *Confessions of a Nazi Spy* made a strong impression on Hitler. The Fuehrer was reportedly so
incensed over the espionage thriller, which deals with a Nazi spy ring thwarted by the FBI, that he planned to
execute Jack Warner once the war was over.

the FBI had set up a shortwave radio station on Long Island so they could listen in on conversations between German spies in New York City and the men they took orders from in Germany.

But even though Clement Derrick was no German spy and sabotage would be ruled out, the sight of the luxurious liner to the stars (she carried William Randolph Hearst, James Stewart, and Sonja Henie on her last crossing) lying on her side like a dead whale was a painful reflection of the U.S. Navy's inability to do its job. In the following weeks, as Americans continued to file past her in what would seem like an endless wake, a *New York Times* editorial summarized their feelings: "The investigation should be relentless. It is not alone a ship that has been damaged. Men may have to die on the other side of some ocean because help cannot get to them in time."

And it was relentless. As newspaper columnists and radio broadcasters kept talk of sabotage very much alive, six different investigations were underway. Even President Roosevelt was not ruling out sabotage, asking his secretary of the Navy immediately after the fire whether any enemy aliens were permitted to work on the ship. Just three days after the fire, the FBI restaged Clement Derrick's lethal accident, bringing the welder and the crew that was with him to an area where they had erected a stanchion similar to the one he was working on at the time of the fire. They surrounded it with bales of burlap and watched as the repeated ballet produced the same terrible result.

Even though the FBI's investigation put to rest the possibility of sabotage, the sight of the destroyed ship's carcass on its side in the Hudson River made New Yorkers question the U.S. Navy's ability to protect the coastline or even the city's waterfront. German U-boats continued to do their deadly mischief off the Long Island and New Jersey beaches. And still the lights of Asbury Park and Atlantic City were shining out toward the sea like welcoming beacons for the enemy.

In March, District Attorney Frank Hogan decided it was time to fight fire with fire. After a meeting with Lieutenant Commander Charles R. Haffenden of the U.S. Office of Naval Intelligence, Hogan

SICILIAN-BORN CHARLES "LUCKY" LUCIANO, one of organized crime's most powerful figures, came to the aid of America during the war years in return for a one-way ticket to Italy. This police mug shot of Luciano shows his drooping right eye, the result of a knife attack that severed the muscles in his right cheek.

set a plan in motion that would utilize the services of one of the most notorious criminals then serving time in upstate New York's Dannemora Prison. Ironically, in 1939 when the *Normandie* was moved from France to New York Harbor to keep her safe, Charles "Lucky" Luciano was sitting in his jail cell hatching a plan with his visitors, mobsters Frank Costello, Meyer Lansky, and Moe Polakoff, to get him released from jail. Part of that plan would involve the *Normandie.* It wasn't until the bombing of Pearl Harbor that Luciano's plan began to take form. Calling his three pals together again, he showed them a newspaper article in which the Navy expressed concern about the possibility of the Germans sabotaging ships in the harbor. It was Luciano's idea to create a "sabotage incident" and then fix it so the U.S. Navy would come to him for help. Luciano would provide that help in exchange for a pardon from the man

who sent him up the river, former prosecutor Thomas Dewey, who had just been elected governor. A month later, Frank Costello paid Luciano another visit, this time letting the mobster know that Albert Anastasia had worked out a scheme with his brother "Tough Tony," a major figure in the International Longshoremen's Association, to do something big that might involve the *Normandie.*

Now, in late March, with the famous

ship destroyed and with Luciano still in jail and believing that Anastasia had carried out his sabotage scheme, a meeting was arranged between the Navy's Haffenden and Joe "Socks" Lanza in the lieutenant's private office off the mezzanine of the Hotel Astor. Lanza reigned over the Fulton Fish Market, and in a burst of patriotism had just agreed to use his mackerel fishing fleet to help ferret out the U-boats plaguing the New York coastal waters. With this handshake agreement, a strange marriage was sanctioned between the U.S. Navy and key players in the New York Mafia. But helpful as Lanza's fishing fleet might be in spotting U-boats, it was not enough. The New York waterfront—especially the West Side docks with their constant gridlock of merchant and troopships—was vital to the country's war effort and it needed protection. The man who controlled it all was Luciano. On May 12, the mobster was removed from Dannemora and brought south to Great Meadow Prison in Comstock, a kinder, gentler place by prison standards. In return for a one-way ticket to Sicily after his sentence was served, Luciano agreed to become the silent arm of Naval Intelligence.

That arm reached beyond the docks into the heart of the city. Yorkville, with the vestiges of the German-American Bund, was still a gravitating spot for German agents who might pick up some vital bits of information in its popular bars. Bartenders became eavesdroppers. Harlem numbers runners and guys who serviced the city's vending machines were turned into informants. That cigarette girl in the nightclub, the hatcheck girl in the restaurant, or the attendant in the powder room might be listening.

It did not last forever, but for a brief period of time when patriotism was the country's unifying glue, the U.S. Navy and the Mafia were partners. Damon Runyon couldn't have written a better script.

JOHN CULLEN delivered furniture for Macy's before joining the U.S. Coast Guard, where he was assigned to the lifeboat station in Amagansett, Long Island.

6

Saboteurs Land in the Hamptons

"There are Germans on the beach. Let's go!"

John Cullen
Seaman, second class, U.S. Coast Guard

It was ten minutes past midnight on June 13, 1942, when John Cullen left the Amagansett Lifeboat Station on the eastern tip of Long Island to begin his patrol. Cullen was a "sand-pounder," the nickname given to U.S. Coastguardsmen assigned to beach patrol. The twenty-one-year-old's job was to walk the beach from his station to the next one at Napeague, just west of the Montauk station, watching for German U-boats. A "pea soup" fog had crept onto the beach and over the sand dunes that hugged this Long Island beachfront community, cutting Cullen's visibility down to a few yards. Making his way east past an observation tower and the

101

Amagansett Naval Radio Station, whose purpose here was to track enemy submarines in the Atlantic, Cullen decided that with the fog so thick, it was best to walk close to the ocean where the sand was firm and smooth. The young guardsman had been walking for about fifteen minutes, covering nearly half a mile, when he saw what appeared to be three figures emerging from the sea carrying a large object. By June of 1942, with the ever-present threat of surfacing U-boats, the beaches along Long Island's coastline were off-limits to civilians at nightfall. Everyone was aware of the regulations. What were these men doing there?

Shining his flashlight at them, Cullen asked that they identify themselves. When one of them stepped forward, claiming they were fishermen who had run aground on their way from East Hampton to Montauk, the Coastguardsman knew something was up. If they were fishing, why had they kept so close to shore? The spokesman for the other two was wearing a fedora and his pants were dripping wet. This was no fisherman. After agreeing to accompany Cullen to the Amagansett Lifeboat Station, the man in the fedora suddenly balked. They didn't have fishing permits, he explained. Just then, a fourth man appeared out of the fog. This one was wearing only a bathing suit and dragging a large canvas sack that was wet from

the ocean. He began to speak in German, a language Cullen didn't know but recognized from war movies. That's when things began to unravel.

"You damn fool!" the English-speaking man shouted. "Why don't you go back to the other guys?"

The man retreated and the English-speaking man suddenly grabbed Cullen's arm.

"Do you have a mother?" he blurted out.

"Yes," a surprised Cullen answered.

"A father?"

Upon the affirmative response the man said, "I wouldn't want to kill you." With that, he reached into a tobacco pouch and pulled out a wad of bills.

Just as Cullen attempted to refuse the bribe, more money came out of the pouch and with it, dialogue right out of a gangster movie:

"Look in my eyes," the English-speaking man said. "Would you recognize me if you saw me again?"

"No," Cullen answered. "I never saw you before in my life."

More convoluted threats ensued and then, after accepting the money to convince the quartet that his silence could be bought, Cullen was allowed to leave. He raced back to the lifeboat station and alerted his boss. The station at Napeague was also notified, and by 1:00 A.M.,

THIS CAPTURED GERMAN U-BOAT is similar to the one that deposited the four saboteurs on a Long Island beach.

Coastguardsmen from both stations were combing the fog-drenched beach for the Germans. Cullen was ordered to return to the spot where he had encountered them. As he waited with two other Coastguardsmen, Cullen caught the smell of diesel fuel floating in from the ocean. The fog was still very thick but as they looked out to sea, Cullen and his colleagues could make out a dark, slender object in the water that was throwing off a blinking light. The sound of an engine now floated in the air. They knew immediately what was out there. What they did not know was that the U-boat that had delivered the Germans across the Atlantic onto the Long Island beach was stuck on a sandbar. The submarine's captain had been so preoccupied with the dinghy used by the sailors who had escorted the saboteurs onto the beach, he hadn't paid sufficient attention to the ebbing tide.

Cullen wasn't the only one to spot the U-boat. The sandbar that had trapped it was just a short distance from the Amagansett Naval Radio Station that Cullen had passed as he began his watch. Inside, Chief Radioman Harry McDonald also smelled the diesel fuel and heard the engines. Convinced that the U-boat had its sights on the station, a frightened McDonald sent his family to stay with friends and closed it down.

Because reports of U-boat sightings up and down the East Coast had now become very frequent and were mostly unfounded, U.S. Naval Intelligence dismissed out of hand the majority of the calls they got. McDonald's experience was no different. When he called the U.S. Coast Guard and the Army's 113th Military Infantry Unit, which happened to be just five miles down the road, each rebuffed him with a bureaucratic "we're not interested." Sadly, the string of lifeboat stations stretching from Maine to Florida were a pathetic excuse for the nation's defense, especially since beach patrols were not constant and guardsmen were unarmed. Ironically, as McDonald was trying to get someone to pay attention, Cullen's boss had spotted a light that had just been turned on in a nearby beach cottage. With the now vigorously enforced blackout, he decided this had to be a signal from an enemy agent to the U-boat. What he didn't know was that at that moment, four German saboteurs (two of whom had already encountered Cullen on the beach) had spotted the same light.

The four were lying low in a patch of scrub grass, close enough to the cottage to hear a telephone ring. The terrified Germans pressed themselves into the wet grass as the man inside answered it. Like the U-boat that brought them here, the saboteurs decided they were trapped. "We're surrounded, boys," one of them said when the light went on, repeating it like a verbal shiver. They also heard the same diesel engine as Cullen and McDonald, but they assumed it meant that their U-boat was on its way back across the Atlantic.

It was now 3:00 in the morning. As Cullen and McDonald were trying to find a way to keep the U-boat from slipping away, its desperate captain had lost all hope of extricating it from the sandbar and was preparing his crew to surrender. Explosives were placed in strategic spots on the sub. Once the crew got on the dinghy he would blow it up. Suddenly, the U-boat began to lift! It was the incoming tide loosening it from the sandbar. One final rev of the engines did the job, and the U-boat that was so close to capture had slipped beyond the reach of the U.S. Navy and Coast Guard.

Meanwhile, the four saboteurs had left the beach area and made their way to the nearby Montauk Highway. The plan was to reach the Long Island Rail Road station at Amagansett, where they would catch a train to Manhattan. Montauk Highway runs east toward Montauk and west in the direction of New York City. As the quartet stood on the highway's edge, it was up to the man in the fedora to decide whether they should turn left or right.

The operation that brought these men from Germany to this summer colony at the tip of Long Island had been, like all things German, carefully planned. It even had a code name: Operation Pastorius, for Franz Daniel Pastorius, the man who brought the first Germans to the New World. The plan was pretty straightforward: Through a series of well-coordinated bombings, vital links to U.S. industry would be destroyed, delivering a crippling blow to the country's ability to wage its war against Germany. Bombs were to be placed under bridges, including the Hell Gate Bridge at the entrance to Long Island Sound. One would be placed in Newark's Pennsylvania Station. There would be bombs inside tunnels serving the Chesapeake

and Ohio Railway—the country's leading transporter of coal. Aluminum plants vital for the production of airplanes would also be bombed. To shake things up, incendiaries would be placed in railroad lockers, Jewish-owned department stores, and other random places, undermining confidence in the country's ability to protect its citizens. The makings of those bombs had been carried to shore in wooden crates by the saboteurs and were now lying where they had been hastily buried in the Amagansett sand. In three days, another four saboteurs would land in Ponte Vedra, Florida, to take part in the same deadly mission.

The four who were now standing alongside the Montauk Highway had been chosen because they each had spent time in the United States. Ernest Burger was a U.S. citizen. The former Storm Trooper came here in 1927 and worked as a machinist in the Midwest. He even joined the National Guard. But in 1933 he went back home, when the prospect of a Germany under Hitler was too compelling to ignore. Both Heinrich Heinck and Richard Quirin had been members of the German-American Bund in Yorkville. George Dasch, the group's leader and the man in the fedora, not only worked in the United States for nineteen years as a salesman and waiter, he had an American-born wife living in New York City.

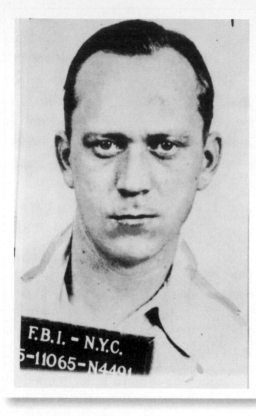

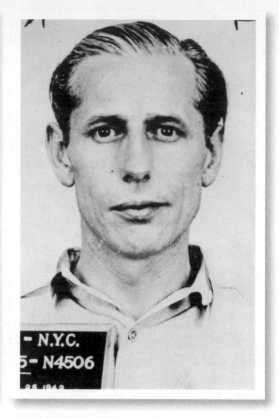

Saboteur HEINRICH HEINCK had been a member of the German-American Bund.

GEORGE DASCH, the leader of the pack, had an American wife living in Manhattan.

From the moment they landed, mishaps plagued the saboteurs. After threatening and bribing Cullen, Dasch joined the other three farther down the beach only to discover that his fresh clothes were still in the spot where he had landed. Retracing his steps, he hurriedly put on the jacket he'd bought at Macy's the last time he was in New York and ordered the men to bury their German navy fatigues in the sand. He had dressed so hastily that as he stood at the edge of the highway in the dark, the man whose clothes were meant to provide camouflage was wearing unmatched socks. Trying to get his bearings, Dasch looked right and then left before making the decision to go to the right. The four men were now heading away from the Amagansett station toward Montauk.

At about the time Dasch was leading his men in the wrong direction, two

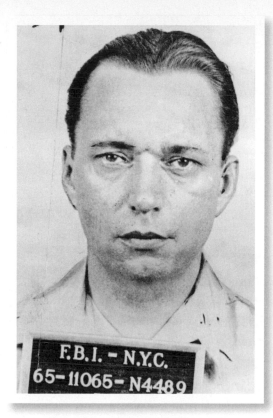

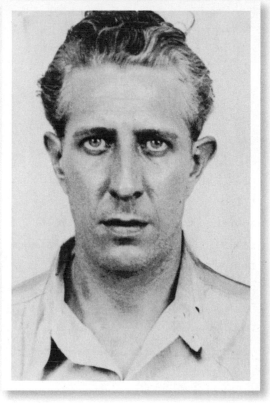

Saboteur ERNEST BURGER was an American citizen working in the Midwest when Hitler's promise of an Aryan nation drew him back to Germany.

Like Heinrich Heinck, RICHARD QUIRIN had been a member of the German-American Bund.

Coast Guard Intelligence officers whom Cullen's boss had persuaded to investigate the site had just arrived from New York City. The four wooden crates and the wet duffel bag with the discarded German uniforms had already been discovered and were now sitting in the boat room of the Amagansett Lifeboat Station, with all the paraphernalia needed to make the bombs spread across the floor.

Dawn was breaking, casting an in-criminating light on Dasch's mistake. Dasch's mismatched socks were the least of the quartet's problems. All four spies were noticeably dirty and disheveled. Burger had a couple of German draft registration cards in his pocket. He had also left a pack of German cigarettes on one of the sand dunes. Dasch reversed directions and corrected his mistake, but not before encountering a campground where vacationers on the site were just waking up to the new day. Once more they expected to be caught, but fate was still giving them a pass, and by 6:00 A.M. they were at the Amagansett railroad station buying four one-way tickets on the 6:59 to New York City.

The train pulled into Jamaica at a few minutes past 9:00. Since they would have to change here for another train to Manhattan, it was a good opportunity to buy some new clothes. Fear of capture was beginning to drop away from them as these men who never knew what it was like to have money were now arriving in New York City, each with $90,000 strapped to his waist. They went on a spending spree, buying the most expensive shirts and ties and gabardine suits they could find in Jamaica, Queens. Dasch suggested they break up in pairs, arriving in the city separately and meeting at the Horn & Hardart Automat into Macy's basement at 3:00 that afternoon.

As they were trying on their new clothes, the wooden crates containing the explosives and the still sodden duffel bag that they thought were buried in the sand were being transported by station wagon to the Coast Guard's Barge Office at the Battery, where they would await the arrival of the FBI.

Quirin and Heinck caught the subway into Manhattan. Wanting to stay separate, Dasch and Burger decided to take the Long Island Rail Road into Pennsylvania Station. It was a hot, humid Saturday and the cavernous railroad station, which usually was crowded with men and women in uniform, was almost empty. June 13, 1942, wasn't just any Saturday. It was the day the city was to hold its New York at War Parade, a massive demonstration of the city's patriotic will. An estimated two and a half million New Yorkers were lining Fifth Avenue from Washington Square to 79th Street, anxious to view the great floats and to hear the patriotic marching bands. The parade had kicked off at noon, and by the time Dasch and Burger were crossing Seventh Avenue to check into the Governor Clinton Hotel, squadrons of airplanes demonstrating the country's military might were flying over the city.

Nostalgia for life in New York came rushing over Dasch as he made his way across the avenue. If he was feeling an emotional tug for the city he had left behind, the man who came here to help bring America to its knees was nearly euphoric when he walked into the Automat. His memories of the unique cafeteria chain with its familiar wall of little glass doors holding delicious pies and sandwiches were very tender. "Aren't you glad to be back in the United States?" he asked Quirin and Heinck, smiling broadly. He had just released two salads and a piece of coconut pie from those windows and had poured himself a tall glass of cold milk.

After agreeing to meet the other two the following day, either at the Swiss Chalet restaurant on West 52nd Street at 1:00 or, if that proved impossible, at Grant's Tomb on Riverside Drive at 6:00, Dasch and Burger did some more shopping for clothes in Macy's and then headed back to their hotel for a bath and a nap. Over steak dinners that night fueled by a bottle of wine, the two men bonded, opening up to one another about the harsh times they each endured under the Gestapo. Later in the evening, with his nostalgia for the city mixing pleasantly with the wine, Dasch led Burger into the summer night. They walked uptown, mingling with the throngs of New Yorkers who had witnessed the war parade, and were headed for Rockefeller Center. Dasch likely couldn't resist taking Burger through Times Square as they made their way to Fifth Avenue and 49th Street. Even with the marquee lights dimmed and the great signs darkened by the recently enforced dim-out, the energy of the city was still palpable and impossible to resist. If they had paused in front of the Rialto on the corner of Broadway and 42nd Street, they would have noticed a newly released movie that would have touched some nerves. *Nazi Agent* featured

Conrad Veidt playing German twins: the good one, a patriotic German-American and the evil twin, a Nazi spy. When they reached Rockefeller Center, Dasch led Burger into the lobby to *American Progress*, the mural painted by José Maria Sert depicting the development of America that John D. Rockefeller commissioned to replace the controversially "socialistic" one done by Mexican artist Diego Rivera. Dasch, who was raised by a socialist mother, focused on the painting's emphasis on a free society as he explained its themes to Burger. The day had been a transforming one for Dasch. It was a little after midnight, just twenty-four hours since he'd emerged from the U-boat and landed on Amagansett's beach, when the exhausted spy said good night to his partner and turned the key to his hotel room.

By the next morning it became obvious that Dasch's complaints against the Gestapo were a prelude to the greater story. Inviting Burger into his room and then locking the door so he couldn't escape, Dasch confessed that his intent from the day he was chosen for the mission was to sabotage it. His aim was to enhance American propaganda getting into Nazi Germany so that more Germans would see the true nature of Nazism. Then, Dasch received a shock. Not only was Burger also here under false pretenses, he had already done things to put the mission in jeopardy. He had deliberately left that pack of cigarettes found on the sand dune. This modern-day Hansel had also scattered pieces of his discarded wet clothing along the beach, making it easy for the Coast Guard to find the boxes containing the explosives.

Now that this odd couple had found each other, they had to figure out what to do next. How should they approach the FBI? These were no highly trained double agents. They were lost souls who had bluffed their way to America posing as spies intent on crippling it. Credibility was going to be a problem. They got so caught up in considering what to do and how to do it, they missed their lunch date with the other two saboteurs and were twenty minutes late for their 6:00 rendezvous at Grant's Tomb.

As soon as they reached the bench where Quirin and Heinck were waiting, it was obvious that things had already begun to come apart. The unhappy twosome were angry about being stood up at the Swiss Chalet. They were also growing suspicious of Dasch and Burger and nervous about the whole operation. They were even at odds about whether to retrieve the boxes of explosives buried in the Amagansett sand. Had Dasch's encounter with Cullen made it too dangerous? Was it safe to remain in Manhattan?

With matters left undecided, they agreed to meet again on Tuesday at the same Automat. Dasch and Burger left the other two and boarded a downtown bus. In Dasch's pocket was the telephone number of the FBI office in New York City. He and Burger got off the bus at 52nd Street and walked over to Madison Avenue and into a hotel lobby. It was ten minutes to eight when Dasch slipped into a phone booth and called the local branch of the FBI. Unfortunately, what should have been the telephone call that brought the saboteurs to justice was so badly handled by Dasch, who lost all credibility by demanding to meet with J. Edgar Hoover, that the message was placed in the "crank cases" file and ignored.

By now, a furious J. Edgar Hoover not only knew about the sabotage plot, he was quickly on the Coast Guard's case. How could they let the U-boat and the German agents slip away?

Dasch and Burger never showed up for the Tuesday meeting at the Automat. The implications of his planned Judas act were weighing heavily on Dasch, and he distracted himself with a thirty-six-hour pinochle game at a club for waiters behind Rockefeller Center, one he had frequented when he lived in the city. On Wednesday morning, an exhausted Dasch finally left the card game. This was also the day when the other four saboteurs who were headed for Ponte Vedra would land safely, their crates of explosives securely buried in the Florida sand.

On Thursday morning, Dasch decided he couldn't wait another day. Leaving the task of facing the other two saboteurs to Burger, he boarded a train in Pennsylvania Station and headed for Washington. On Friday, he tried once more to reach Hoover at FBI Headquarters. Serendipitously, he was connected to Duane L. Traynor, an agent who just happened to head the Bureau's anti-sabotage unit. By now President Roosevelt had been informed of the plot, and the U.S. Coast Guard was put on special alert for more possible landings.

Back in New York, Burger, Quirin, and Heinck spent Saturday, their last day of freedom in America, like typical friends enjoying a day in the city. Before meeting the other two for lunch at the Old Oxford restaurant in the Grand Central area, Burger went to Rogers Peet, the men's clothing store on Fifth Avenue and 42nd Street, and bought himself a sharkskin suit. Quirin and Heinck visited the newsreel theater in Grand Central Terminal and watched coverage of the previous Saturday's New York at War Parade. There was some talk of spending Sunday at Coney Island or New Jersey's Palisades Amusement Park before the two parted company with Burger.

Quirin was the first to be arrested as he strolled up Amsterdam Avenue and 76th Street. Heinck had just left a nearby delicatessen when the FBI nabbed him. Burger was arrested in his hotel room, the sharkskin suit still draped over a chair. Three days later, FBI agents picked up two of the Florida group as they were leaving a bar on Lexington Avenue and 42nd Street. The following Saturday, the last two were arrested in Chicago.

On June 28, the *New York Times* announced the news in bold headlines, taking up the entire front page with the story: *FBI Seizes 8 Saboteurs Landed By U-Boats Here And In Florida To Blow Up War Plants.* That same night Walter Winchell took to the airwaves, praising the FBI's work and describing it as "the most exciting achievement of John Edgar Hoover's G-men." Six weeks later, on August 8, six of the saboteurs were executed in Washington's District of Columbia jail. Dasch and Burger were sent to prison, where they would languish until 1948, when they were packed off to Germany. But there was little cause to gloat. It was apparent to the Army, the Navy, the Coast Guard, and the FBI that this bold invasion was thwarted by nothing more than sheer luck.

PART III

THE WAY WE WERE DURING THE WAR

New Yorkers Roll Up Their Sleeves

ONLY THE TIP OF HER TORCH CAN BE
seen as Lady Liberty guards the harbor
in darkness.

Turn Out Those Lights!

"Times Square was the world's window on the American personality, its barometer of the American spirit. To dim those lights, of all the lights in the country, was symbolically to hush the soul of a nation."

Signs and Wonders: The Spectacular Marketing of America
Edward Hayman and Tama Starr, 1998

It had to happen. For months, the entire eastern coastline, from Maine to Florida, had glowed in the dark. Stores, homes, movie theaters, and streetlights helped to turn the Atlantic Ocean into one big shooting gallery. By March 1942, fifty-four freighters and tankers directly off the coastline had been sent to the bottom of the sea, some with their entire crew. And this was just one part of the U-boats' devastating tally. Already, lights at the entrance to New York Harbor were being turned off. In January, the Scotland Lightship, just east of Sandy Hook at the entrance to the Narrows, went dark. So did the Fire Island Lightship, ten miles southwest of the Fire Island Lighthouse. A line of buoys was placed between Ambrose Channel and East Rockaway Inlet, forcing ships to circumvent Ambrose Lightship.

With so much of the country's ship traffic passing along the New Jersey shore, by the middle of the month the state's oceanfront towns, including Asbury Park and Atlantic City, had finally, on orders from the state's Defense Council, dimmed their lights. The dim-out extended ten miles inland, with all lights facing the ocean blacked out. Asbury Park's famous Steel Pier went dark. Along Atlantic City's boardwalk all street lamps were dimmed, with the sides facing the ocean painted black. Desperate to keep tourists coming, the city council installed mauve-tinted bulbs along the boardwalk to encourage a "carnival spirit." Strollers were not permitted to smoke cigarettes: that burning tip could signal a waiting U-boat. Hotel windows with sought-after ocean views had their shades drawn at night, with strict instructions to guests that they were not to raise them. Movie-house marquees were darkened, with only a single light bulb in the cashier's booth providing illumination. "Very romantic" is what Atlantic City's Mayor Tom Taggart said of his darkened playground-by-the-sea. What else could he say?

A few days later, Long Island's South Shore, with its ribbon of beaches stretching from Montauk to Coney Island, went dim. Long Beach, Atlantic Beach, Brighton Beach, and the grand tiara of amusement parks, Coney Island, were now in shadow. And there was Manhattan, the glittering diamond necklace that dazzled in the night sky. Its glow was so intense that a passenger on a ship's deck thirty miles out at sea would recognize it. An airplane flying in darkness could spot the city two hundred miles away. If an enemy wanted to destroy New York City, all he had to do was follow the lights. But convincing New Yorkers to live out the duration of the war in darkness was a tough sell. It would take the U.S. Army to flip the switch.

On April 27 the order was given, and at sundown the following night New York City, along with every community facing the Atlantic Ocean from Maine to Florida, went dim. New Yorkers looking up at their famous skyscrapers that night could no longer find their crowns. The unlit Chrysler and Empire State buildings were lost in the low haze. Without the lamps atop the Time-Life and Associated Press buildings casting their glow onto the RCA Building, 30 Rockefeller Center resembled a cold granite tombstone, and the clocks atop Metropolitan Life and the Paramount Building no longer had faces. Cleaning women working through the night in offices above the fifteenth floor had to clean in dim light with shades drawn. Commuters on the Staten Island Ferry could no longer look out at

the entrance to New York Harbor and see the Statue of Liberty's lighted torch. Passengers on Pennsylvania Railroad trains coming in from New England or entering the tunnel under the Hudson River never saw the city into which they were arriving. Shades in every car were tightly drawn. And when they entered Pennsylvania Station's magnificent skylit Concourse, every pane of glass was painted black. So were the tops of the glass light globes that illuminated the station.

Two days later, the city's heart went dark when Times Square's "spectaculars," the great neon signs that gave the square its life, were turned off. The block-long Wrigley aquarium with its colorful angelfish and veil-tail fighting fish swimming in the night sky, the cascade of Planter's peanuts unceasingly spilling from their bag, the quartet of sprouting red roses heralding Four Roses whiskey, the white bubbles spilling out of the Bromo-Seltzer bottle into the nine-foot glass, the Chevrolet and Coca-Cola signs, and the giant Bond clothing sign with its dependable clock imbedded in the letter "O" were all dark. Theater marquees could no longer be lit; incandescent light bulbs beneath the marquees were all theatergoers had to remind themselves that they were walking the streets of the Great White Way. It was a melancholy irony. This gaudy centerpiece in the country's most

tion. There was a war on, after all, and every New Yorker had to do his or her share. The Astor Theatre beneath the hotel and the nearby Paramount Theater both installed blue light bulbs to soften the glare. The color red was a particular problem. Childs cafeteria on West 44th Street and the Robotti Accordion Academy a few blocks north were among the storefronts that had to banish their red neon signage. Even the lighted globe dropping from the Times Building on New Year's Eve would be put in storage for the war's duration, replaced by a series of chimes. With the exception of the *New York Times* electric news zipper, whose 14,800 bulbs lit up the headlines as they wound around the building, all of Times Square was dimmed.

It was still not enough. Sailors on a Navy patrol boat off Ambrose Light at the mouth of the Narrows could still see a strong incandescent glow cast off from the city's lights. A U-boat could easily find its prey. A bomber could find its target. Now,

vibrant city was supposed to provide an incandescent distraction to the soldiers and sailors on leave or preparing to go off to their training camps. Now with its lights dimmed, Times Square would remind them of what they were heading into.

In spite of protests from the area's merchants—some of whom knew their businesses could not survive the dim-out—compromise was out of the ques-

Mayor La Guardia had to impose more stringent dim-out rules on a city that refused to share his fear of enemy attack. On the last night in April, the entire city went dark as the mayor ordered a citywide blackout. It lasted only twenty minutes, but in that short period of time he was able to take the fear temperature of the city, and the results were not all to his liking. He was pleased with Harlem. Sitting in the backseat of his radio car as John Peluso drove him along 125th Street, the mayor took pride in seeing that every light was out and every person off the street. "The conduct of the people was fine," he boasted to reporters interviewing him in the 54th Street station house.

Then he was told about the thousands who had thronged Times Square to witness the city in darkness, cheering and clapping as the lights went out. The crowd included sailors and soldiers, most of them American, but also British, Australian, and Dutch whose ships were being resupplied at the Brooklyn Navy Yard. They had all gathered to witness the most unnatural sight in the Western world: Times Square lit by nothing but the moon. That night,

THE EMPIRE STATE Building is barely visible in this photograph of 34th Street looking west. The Third Avenue el station can be seen in the foreground.

THE GREAT WHITE WAY IS hardly recognizable during the citywide dim-out. One can barely make out the statue of Father Duffy in front of the darkened Pepsi-Cola Serviceman's Center.

as the dim-out grew dimmer. Everyone had to do better. Although visitors were still permitted in the observatories of the darkened Empire State and RCA buildings, the observatory atop the Woolworth Building was placed off-limits because of its proximity to the Brooklyn Navy Yard. The thirty-two-story Federal Building's gold-leaf pyramidal roof was painted black to prevent its glimmering in moonlight. Stores with awnings were told to keep them lowered at night. Con Edison began testing a dim-out curtain for store windows. Ads appeared in all the city papers for "Permo" blackout shades. For sixty-nine cents these shades, made of something called "blackKraft" paper, would keep the air-raid warden from rapping on your door. Another firm—the

the moon happened to be strong, its yellow glow lighting the sides of the buildings and skimming over the surface of the Hudson and East rivers. "A bomber's moon," one airman shouted to the curious crowd. La Guardia was furious. "We're not going to have a wholesale slaughter," he barked, reminding reporters of the Londoners who perished in the first raid on their city.

"Sky glow" became the operative term

Defense Blackout & Camouflage Company, operating out of the Graybar Building—had gotten into the business early, anticipating the worst. They designed asbestos gloves and goggles and came up with a special blackout paint. Once war came to New York City, their clients included the Rockefeller Institute, Memorial Hospital, the Cosmopolitan Club, and St. John's Church.

Traffic lights were covered in metal masks with narrow slits for the red and green signals to show through. Along Broadway, from the Battery to Washington Heights, every other streetlight was blacked out and the ones left on glowed with less intensity. Car and taxi headlights would soon wear hoods or "eyelids" so that the light they cast would shine down. In the trolleys that made their way through Times Square, a passenger reading a newspaper had to get used to light bulbs that had been dipped in black paint with just the necks exposed. To compensate for the low light, trolley ceilings were painted white. Straphangers entering the ornate IRT kiosks had to make their way down the stairs without lights. Once in the subway cars they had an even more difficult time reading newspapers, since the cars that traveled mostly in dark subway tunnels had the tips of their overhead lights dipped in black paint as well. The only things subway riders could read were advertisements and the placards above the seats telling them what to do in case of an air raid. Those same signs were in trolley cars and elevated trains. Everywhere, New Yorkers saw reminders of their vulnerability. Then, at midnight on Sunday, May 18, people standing around the Times Tower, looking up at the fourth floor where the familiar electric news zipper circled the building, read the bulletin they already knew was coming:

THE NEW YORK TIMES
BIDS YOU GOODNIGHT

In an instant, the lighted sign that had acted as the city's town crier since 1928, informing New Yorkers of FDR's election, Hitler's rise and France's fall, and the burning of the *Normandie* just a few blocks away, went dark. Frank Powell, one of the three electricians who had set the letters in lights every day since the sign's debut in 1928, exclaimed, "All I want is to start it up again the night Hitler gets killed. That would tickle me to death."

It was nearly summer, the first in the city since the war's beginning. For New Yorkers toiling in hot stores, offices, and the new war plants without air-cooling, a night watching the Dodgers at Ebbets Field or the Giants at the Polo Grounds was a promise of sweet relief. (There were no night games at Yankee Stadium, because the ballpark had not yet been

CITY OF NEW YORK
AIR RAID INSTRUCTIONS

WHEN YOU HEAR — Steady note of siren for 2 minutes — **AIR RAID IS PROBABLE**
(1) All building lights blacked out. Keep radio on.
(2) Pedestrians and vehicle movement permitted
(3) Prepare to seek cover.

WHEN YOU HEAR — Warbling note of siren for 2 minutes — **RAIDERS OVERHEAD**
(1) All lights blacked out. Keep radio on.
(2) Vehicles stop, discharge passengers
(3) Everybody take cover.

WHEN YOU HEAR — Steady note of siren for 2 minutes — **RAIDERS MAY RETURN**
(1) Building lights remain blacked out. Keep radio on.
(2) Pedestrians leave cover.
(3) Resume pedestrian and vehicular movement.

WHEN YOU HEAR — Radio broadcast announcement "All Clear" and long blast on police and wardens' whistles. — **RAIDERS HAVE PASSED**
(1) Resume normal activities. All lights on.

REMAIN CALM.   WALK, DO NOT RUN.   OBEY INSTRUCTIONS OF POLICE AND WARDENS.

Effective Feb. 17, 1943

F. H. LaGUARDIA
Mayor

AIR WARDEN SERVICE
POLICE EMERGENCY DIVISION, CITY OF NEW YORK

SIGNS LIKE THIS ONE instructing riders on what to do in case of an air raid were posted in all subway cars, trolleys, and city buses.

equipped with lights.) More than relief, a ballpark was an oasis of normalcy where, for a few hours, war had never been declared. Because most New Yorkers had daytime jobs, attendance at night games was five times greater than those held on weekday afternoons. Fans were anticipating the first night game of the season, scheduled for May 22 at the Polo Grounds, when the New York Giants would play against the Brooklyn Dodgers. Then on May 18, just four days before the game, New York's police commissioner, Lewis J. Valentine, made the announcement that everyone knew was coming: night baseball was out for the next few seasons. Instead, New Yorkers would get "twi-night" games, which would begin before sunset and end no later than one hour after the sun disappeared from the western sky.

It wasn't only baseball. Because of the fear of sabotage from U-boats, all of the city's beaches had a 9:00 p.m. curfew. Jones Beach, Jacob Riis Park, Coney Island, Rockaway Beach, and all the beaches along Long Island's South Shore were totally off-limits at night. No more beach parties. No more night fishing. Even a solitary stroll was off-limits. Beaches along New Jersey's shore, including Asbury Park and Atlantic City, had the same rules.

A month before the citywide dim-out the mayor, who was determined to keep his city in a state of readiness, ordered sporadic blackouts in every neighborhood in every borough. The first twenty-minute blackout, on March 19, covered the twelve miles of Atlantic coastline from Sea Gate, at the western end of Coney Island, to Far Rockaway, on the Nassau County border. It was this band of lights that guided the first U-boat to the tip of Manhattan just a few months before. Staten Island was next, with the blackout occurring on the kind of hazy night that bombers favor. On the following night, the tip of Manhattan went dark, and a few nights after that it was the Bronx's turn.

By late spring, as the ongoing dim-outs, punctuated by the occasional blackouts, became part of the fabric of New York life, the city's "can do" spirit surfaced. Bloomingdale's, one of several department stores with their own air-raid equipment sections, began featuring blackout shades with decorative patterns. Interior designers were getting into the act, suggesting ruffled black drapes to substitute for plain blackout shades.

In Times Square, sign designer Jacob Starr found a novel way to create light. He took thousands of one-inch-square glass mirrored tiles and fashioned them into giant displays. The colored mirrors, which caught and reflected ambient light, made their debut as a giant movie poster for *The Pride of the Yankees,* the story of Lou Gehrig. In the summer of 1942, the Pepsi-Cola sign above the newly installed USO Center got the same treatment, its patriotic shades of red, white, and blue shimmering not only in the square's dim light but in daylight as well. It was this notion of having his signs function equally well in daylight that made designer Douglas Leigh, affectionately called the "Sign King," come up with his famous Camel cigarette sign, stretching the length of a city block from 43rd to 44th Street across the façade of the Claridge hotel. In June of 1941, nearly a year before the dim-out, those memorable ten-foot smoke rings (they were actually produced by steam) drifted across the square every four seconds. When the country went to war, the

PATRIOTISM WAS IN EVIDENCE in this version of "Sign King" Douglas Leigh's Camel billboard showing a U.S. airman blowing those famous smoke rings across Times Square.

Camel man became a soldier, then a sailor, and finally an airman. Knowing the city would endure blackouts once Pearl Harbor was bombed, Leigh devised a way to hook up his seventeen spectaculars to one master switch controlled either from his office or from a spot "somewhere on Broadway." Mayor La Guardia was de-

lighted with the notion that all of Broadway could be turned off with the flick of a switch, but after April 29, 1942, that switch would remain in an "off" position for the duration of the war.

New Yorkers were getting accustomed to the way their city looked and felt during this first year of the war. By Christmas, a trio of Norway spruces brought in from Huntington, Long Island, were installed in Rockefeller Center's Lower Plaza. No one complained when the traditional lights were replaced by red, white, and blue ornaments. And, as a symbol of regeneration and renewal during these dark days, or perhaps as a gesture of the need to conserve, a new tradition was begun: for the next several years, after the giant trees had helped New Yorkers through each of the city's wartime Christmas seasons, they were replanted in their original beds.

If Times Square was the city's release valve during the war years, Rockefeller Center, with its seasonal gardens and skating rink, its boulevard of shops, its Center Theater featuring live ice shows, and its spectacular observation roof, would become a land-bound lighthouse, drawing visitors and New Yorkers as each season was ushered in with celebration. After the Rockefeller Center Choristers packed away their Christmas-carol song sheets and the trio of trees were trucked back to Long Island, ice skaters and shivering strollers could look forward to spring, when the Channel Gardens were filled with beds of Easter lilies. Rockefeller Center was just two years old when Pearl Harbor was bombed, but those twenty-two acres of dazzling art deco architecture and generous public spaces emanated a sense of permanence in a time that was so very uncertain.

ALL OF NEW YORK CITY turned out for the massive New York at War Parade.

Shining Through

*Even in the darkest days of the war
there was an optimism in the city.
We knew we were going to win.*

Ethel Ursprung

It was December 31, 1941, the first New Year's
Eve to be celebrated in Times Square since war was declared. All
day long there was a certain feeling in the air, an almost universal
urgency among New Yorkers to let the world know that America
was not going to be defeated. What better time to make that clear
than on the eve of resolutions, and what better place than here at
the Crossroads of the World? Anyone taking odds on how New
Yorkers would welcome this New Year had only to call the State
Liquor Authority, which reportedly got over two thousand requests
for special all-night licenses from bars around the city. Grand

Twenty-eight Exit Routes Mapped for New Yorkers

Here are the routes civilians can use in leaving the City, in case the Army takes over the main highways. All civilian roads carry a number in the 500s. Markers have been placed every two miles and at all important intersections. The map is by the Metropolitan Defense Transport Comm.

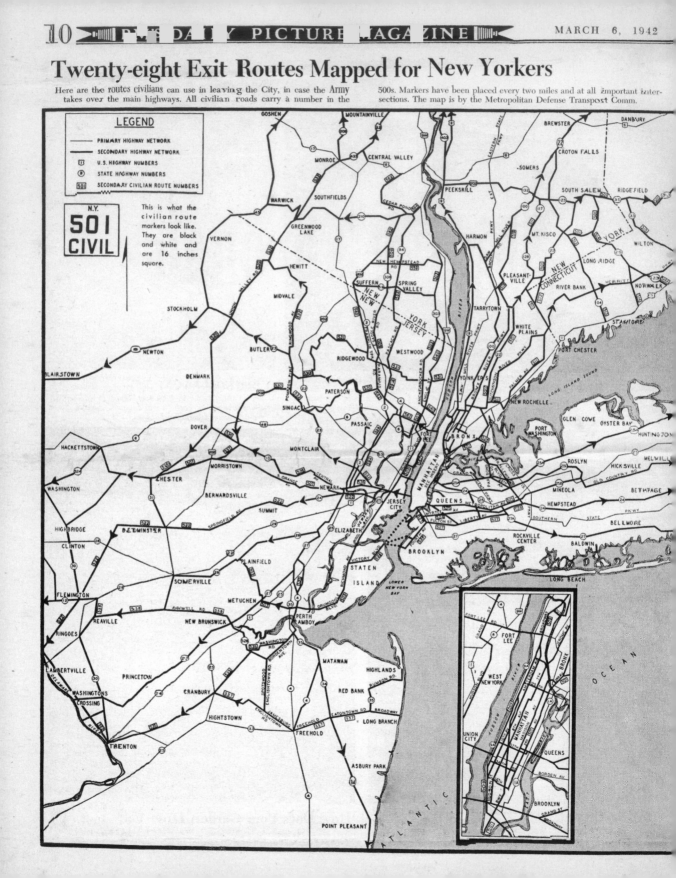

Central Terminal's Oyster Bar stocked up on one hundred thousand oysters for its famous "Hangover Stew." The city's hospitals, including nearby St. Clare's on Ninth Avenue and 51st Street, kept their emergency rooms fully staffed in preparation for the anticipated stream of New Yorkers who might celebrate a little too injudiciously.

By 5:00 that evening, the bar at the Commodore Hotel—considered among serious drinkers to be the world's longest at 165 feet—could not accommodate the customers who were already standing eight feet deep. In desperation, the hotel manager installed a bartender behind the counter of the hotel's coffee shop and brought in a rumba band to mollify the thirsty crowd. The city's biggest hotels—the Biltmore, the Astor, and the Savoy-Plaza among them—had been solidly booked for weeks. All of the private and public dining and entertaining rooms at the Waldorf-Astoria, including the Grand Ballroom and Starlight Roof, would be filled, with no fewer than twelve orchestras ready to play into the New Year. The Copa, El Morocco, the Stork Club—every nightclub in the city—was jammed

to capacity. Even the Aviation Terrace and the Kitty Hawk Room at La Guardia Field had no empty tables. Roseland was already packed with soldiers and sailors, and up at the Rainbow Room atop Rockefeller Center, the National Broadcasting Company was getting ready to go live with a broadcast of this first New Year with America at war.

As revelers from Brooklyn, the Bronx, Queens, and Staten Island were emerging from subway stations and spilling into Times Square, they were joined by the soldiers and sailors whose presence would soon be a constant in the city. Those from Australia and Scotland were surprised and delighted by the crowd's exuberance. Vendors were also delighted to see their tin horns and noisemakers being swooped up. So were Times Square's familiar flower ladies, who quickly sold out of their orchid and gardenia corsages. The crowds continued to gather, bathed in the incandescent lights of the Crossroads of the World. There was no dim-out yet and all the theater marquees and penny arcades were blinking away while high above the square, the giant electric billboards blazed into the night. On this New Year's Eve, Times Square looked the way it had before America was at war. Even the predicted rain never materialized. For those New Yorkers who worried about an air raid, the clearing skies were a good sign.

ON MARCH 6, 1942, *PM MAGAZINE* PUBLISHED THIS map indicating routes New Yorkers should use to leave the city in the event of an air attack.

If Hitler's planes ever did make it to their city, they were told that they would choose to fly under cloud cover. Tonight's sky was cloudless and lit by a full moon.

Even with the threat of an air raid on Times Square a remote possibility, Mayor La Guardia and his police commissioner, Lewis J. Valentine, were taking no chances. By 7:00, fire trucks were positioned in front of the Times Tower on 43rd Street and around Father Duffy's statue a few blocks north on 46th Street. Loudspeakers were hoisted on lampposts so evacuation instructions could be given. More than two thousand policemen—many from the other boroughs—were filing into the square. Three hours later, sixteen hundred air-raid wardens emerged from the east ballroom of the Hotel Astor, having just been briefed on their duties. They quickly took their positions beneath traffic and street lamps whose globes had already been painted black at the top. In the event of an air raid, the wardens' instructions were to immediately switch off the lights. Signs were posted on lampposts at every intersection instructing people where to go once the sirens rang out. A sign on the Paramount Theater's marquee sought to reassure its customers: *The New York Paramount is thoroughly prepared for any emergency. Our well-trained staff of 160 has been drilled to maintain the safety of its patrons at all times.*

By 11:30, Broadway's theaters had all let out and playgoers who had just seen *Panama Hattie*, *Arsenic and Old Lace*, and *My Sister Eileen* joined the throng now estimated to be above 500,000. If one counted the crowds spilling over the periphery of the square, there were one million people gathered here tonight to help ring in the New Year. Bill Shaw, a Hell's Kitchen resident whose vaudevillian parents worked the Palace, was in Times Square that night: "My brother was wearing his Civil Defense hat with the big red cross on the top of it. Times Square was a sea of people. We were shoulder-to-shoulder." Eighteen-year-old Brooklyn resident Evelyn Margulies remembers, "It was so crowded, my coat was practically ripped off me. It was very exciting." Anne King was worried that the crowd would tempt pickpockets. She says, "I put my boyfriend's wallet in my bra." With all eyes focused on the Times Tower where the famous ball was poised to drop, a reminder of where history had placed the city on this night crept across the lighted zipper as news of Japan's imminent invasion of Manila circled the building. Behind the crowds at the northern end of the square, a sign in red and blue bold letters on the former Studebaker Building read: *Remember Pearl Harbor! Buy Defense Bonds.*

Pearl Harbor was precisely what was on the minds of these New Yorkers as they waited for the New Year to ring in. This was not a night of forgetfulness, but one of commitment to a cause that was, in their hearts and minds, entirely winnable. As these revelers were celebrating, war plants in the New York area were already operating all through the night. On the bulletin board of one of the plants a worker had tacked a sign: *Let's give the New Year's Day headache to Hitler instead of ourselves. Remember Pearl Harbor. Remember Manila. Every man at his place on New Year's Day with a clear head.*

As the ball was about to descend, Lucy Monroe, a young soprano who was often called upon to sing at the city's ball games and patriotic rallies, began the first bars of the "Star-Spangled Banner." A momentary hush settled on the crowd and then they joined in, 500,000 strong as the country's national anthem resounded across the square. Servicemen were hoisted on the shoulders of civilians as the ball began to drop. At the stroke of midnight, as the numbers "1942" were switched on and blazed across the sky, the crowd let out a roar that echoed off the buildings and into the microphones of the radio networks stationed here. Giant klieg lights illuminated the square as cars and taxis and ships in the harbor blared their horns. And across the nation, people tuning in to their radios could hear the way New York City was ringing in 1942.

It was just three weeks since war had been declared, and New York City was brimming with patriotic zeal. Now, when Mayor La Guardia warned of the war coming "right to our streets and residential districts," New Yorkers listened. Actually, on May 12, 1942, a few months after the mayor spoke those words of gloom, German engineers were actively working on an "Amerika Bomber," also known as the "New York Bomber." According to Manfred Griehl, author of *Luftwaffe Over America*, "Hitler . . . imagined New York 'going down in a sea of flames'. He visualized the skyscrapers as gigantic 'towers of flame' and as 'blazing bundles of firewood'. . . . [and] Manhattan, a 'bursting city', [which] would provide a foretaste of Dante's Inferno." The German plan was to fly a four-engine plane carrying a light bomber beneath its fuselage across the Atlantic. Once the plane came within sight of the New York City skyline, the smaller bomber would be released to deliver its payload. The pilot would then ditch his plane into the ocean, where a waiting U-boat would rescue him. So intent were the Germans on bombing this symbolic city, they drew up a detailed map of Manhattan with an arrow pointing to its center.

Even if they knew nothing of the German bombing scheme, New Yorkers understood that they were dealing with a very real threat. One had only to pick up a newspaper and look at the photos of bomb-ravaged London or listen to Edward R. Murrow's radio broadcasts from that devastated city to know how vulnerable this skyscraper metropolis would be if Hitler's planes could get over here. By November 1941, a month before Pearl Harbor, La Guardia

had signed up 109,000 volunteer air-raid wardens and 60,000 Fire Department auxiliaries. Now, in this first week of the New Year, the mayor had 212,000 volunteers. By the end of January, that number would grow to a quarter of a million as

SIX MONTHS BEFORE the attack on Pearl Harbor, Mayor La Guardia was urging New Yorkers to volunteer for civil defense. Here he poses with Eleanor Roosevelt and a model wearing the new apron designed for female civil defense workers.

volunteers from every borough signed up.

New York City was now in a state of readiness. Everyone from elevator boys in apartment buildings to ferryboat captains plying the Hudson River had a role in the city's air defense. Volunteer guards reinforced the regular employees who protected the Holland and Lincoln tunnels and all of the city's bridges. The Empire State Building, with its eight thousand tenants, had monitors and assistant monitors on every floor drilled in getting their people to the halls and stairwells in the event of an air raid. At Rockefeller Center, nine thousand sandbags along with forty-gallon tanks of water were distributed to tenants to put out fires from incendiary bombs. Macy's put an elaborate system into place. At the sound of the alarm, all store windows would go dark and "blackout wings" would be drawn across exit doors to prevent light from seeping out as wardens directed customers to safety. A registered nurse presided over the store's emergency hospital while the emergency repair crew slipped into rubber suits and asbestos gloves in case of fire. In apartment buildings, tenants were asked to designate certain floors they considered to be safest from attack to house residents in an emergency. Blackout posters with instructions on what to do in case of an air raid were on the walls of most office and apartment buildings.

Air-raid drills became part of everyone's life. Once a week, when the sirens went off, thousands of air-raid wardens in every borough donned helmets, grabbed flashlights and badges, and walked the streets of their neighborhoods making sure that the blocks they patrolled were in total darkness. Brooklyn resident Doris Lipetz remembers them well: "We had to turn off our lights and draw down the shades. Most of our neighbors went downstairs and stood in front of their houses." Joan Harris, who grew up in Bensonhurst, was terrified that these drills were prelude to a real attack: "We pulled down our blackout curtains and sat frozen around the kitchen table." Jackson Heights was always a very proactive community. As soon as war was declared they had put their own plan into place, and by January their air-raid drills were exquisitely choreographed ballets that included volunteer house wardens, first-aid and fire wardens, and roof wardens whose job it was to search for approaching enemy planes.

Those roof wardens were part of a larger group of volunteer airplane "spotters" scattered throughout the five boroughs, whose job it was to report on the flights on any given night in the skies over the city. As early as January 1941, a full year before the attack on Pearl Harbor, ten observation posts were designated across the metropolitan area. Equipped with a

Telephone operators would then refer to huge table maps to verify the positions of planes in question. There were posts on Staten Island, in Brooklyn, Queens, the Bronx, and Manhattan, where a few volunteers got to search for enemy planes atop the eighty-sixth-floor Observation Deck of the Empire State Building. Former governor Al Smith, who had been a force in getting the city's tallest skyscraper built and had had little else to do since then except to escort foreign dignitaries to the Observation Deck, now thoughtfully

pair of army-regulation binoculars, a chart of incoming and outgoing flights, and a nearby telephone connected to the Army Interceptor Command's nerve center located on the twelfth floor of the New York Telephone Company Building on West Street, the men and women who manned the posts would identify each aircraft that appeared in the sky against a list, reporting on any plane that was not scheduled to be in the air that night.

BY CHRISTMAS 1942, NEW YORKERS WERE actively involved in civil defense efforts. This Macy's salesclerk is selling books on civil defense.

installed a shower stall and a locker on the eighty-first floor. A good supply of coffee was always on hand.

Bomb drills were held in every neighborhood. On February 4, the quiet streets of Manhattan's elegant Sutton Place were roused when an air-raid patrol car raced from block to block, pausing so its air-raid warden could jump out and douse phantom incendiaries. Up on the Grand Concourse, a trial being held in the Bronx County Building was interrupted when alarms went off, signaling an air-raid drill. Air-raid drills and air-raid sirens, air-raid instruction posters and air-raid shelters now became part of every New Yorker's daily life. "You were constantly reminded of the war," remembers photographer Arthur Leipzig. "There was no way to avoid it." By early spring, the American Red Cross had designated over a thousand sites in all five boroughs as emergency relief centers. In the event of an attack, the centers, located in schools, churches, clubs, and dance halls, were stocked with cots,

I was in elementary school, ready to go into junior high. We would go into the hall as a class and sit along the sides of the walls. We would have to cover our heads.

—NORMA BOCK

I remember they taped all the windows in our school with white tape crosswise and on the diagonal.

—PHILLIP CURTIN

food, and clothing in order to care for the newly homeless and injured. Even nightly visiting hours in the city's hospitals were eliminated so that, in the event of a night raid, the hospital staff could care for the bombing victims.

The mayor lost no time in dealing with the issue of the city's schoolchildren. A week after Pearl Harbor, every public, private, and parochial school in the city had received instructions on what to do in case of an air raid. By January air raid drills were part of the school week, and in February special ID tags were distributed to every student. Norma Bock remembers, "We wore these round discs to school with our names and identification on them. You put them on a cord or a chain and wore them around your neck. It gave us a certain sense of security. It always reminded me that something was going on." Marlene, another young girl, had a different reaction: "We'd make these mats out of oilcloth and stuff them with cotton. We'd use them to sit on whenever there was an air-raid drill. I was always very scared."

As each month drew the country deeper into war, there was talk of evacuating the city's children and housing them in vacant summer homes in the Hamptons and upper Westchester. For many boys and girls, however, leaving their city behind while adults helped with the war effort was the last thing they wanted to do. *New York Times* reporter Catherine Mackenzie interviewed some city kids for "Need to be Needed," a feature that appeared on December 6, 1942,

We all had to wear them. The first thing your teacher would ask was, "Do you have your ID tag?"

—EDNA SATENSTEIN

about children who wanted to pitch in. "We could learn to watch for airplanes if they would trust us," said one eleven-year-old boy. "I would like to be a messenger but they say I'm not old enough," said another. Ironically, as early as 1940 the New York City school system had responded to the war, teaching the principles of American democracy versus Germany's Nazism in social studies classes. Vocational training in high school was stepped up, and science classes often included the making of an incendiary bomb. Aviation, navigation, and the deployment of troops became familiar examples in solving math problems. For elementary school children, simple math could include "Two

THESE BOYS playing war games in a Brooklyn lot are alleviating their own fears about the war while having fun.

THIS CLASS AT BENJAMIN Franklin High School are learning the basic principles of first aid.

Edna Colligan
5-13-31
24-13164NYC

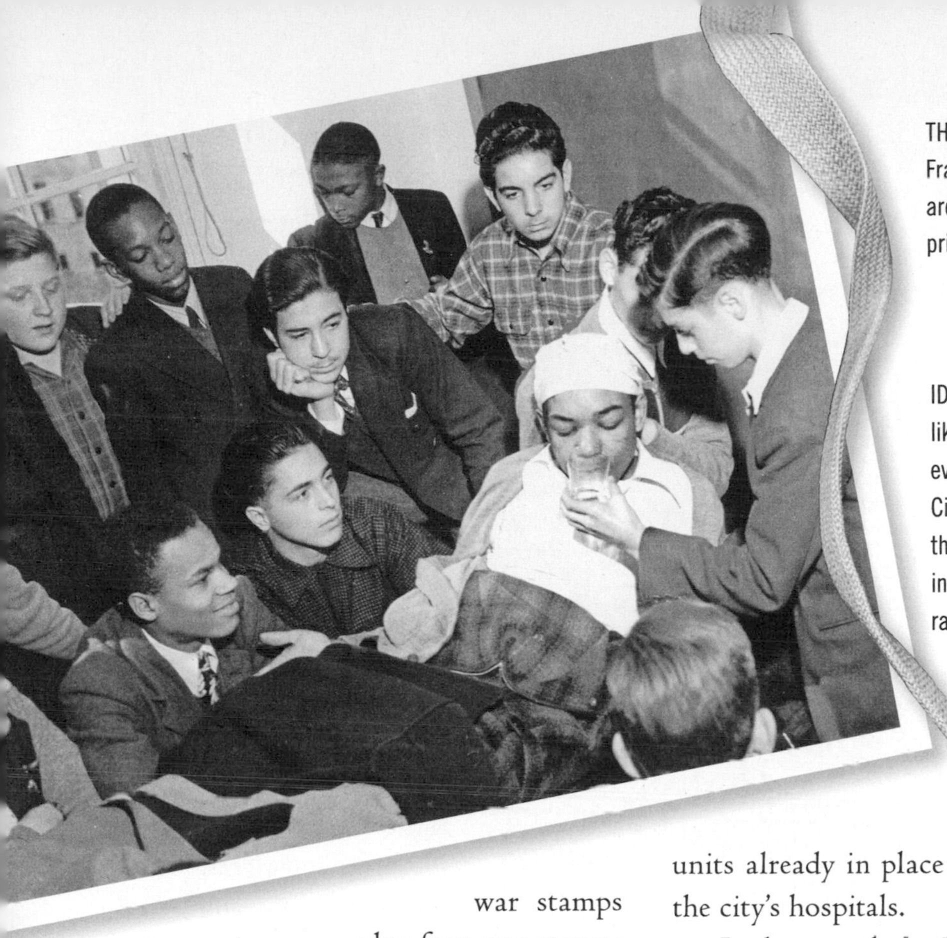

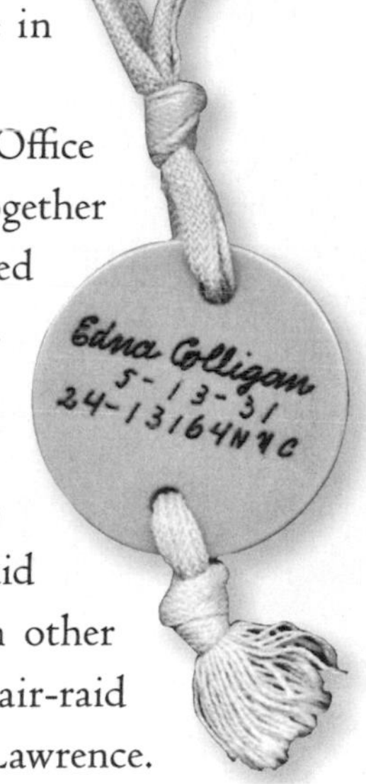

IDENTIFICATION TAGS like this one were worn every day by New York City schoolchildren so they could be identified in the event of an air raid attack.

war stamps plus four war stamps equals how many war stamps?”

With all this planning for the possibility that enemy bombs might fall on New York City, psychiatrists were concerned about the mental health of the city’s children. In January 1942, a group of prominent psychiatrists formed the New York Society for Child Psychiatry with headquarters at the Payne Whitney Clinic of New York Hospital. In addition to training air-raid wardens, teachers, and even parents on how to avert panic among the young, these psychiatrists volunteered for the emergency medical units already in place in the city’s hospitals.

In that month the Office of Civilian Defense, together with the American Red Cross and the Girl Scouts, began training girls between the ages of fourteen and eighteen in intensive first-aid courses. Boys took on other jobs. “I was a junior air-raid warden,” said David Lawrence. “I painted little triangles with stripes on old tin hats the British had used. Once a month when there was a drill, my buddies and I would go through

AIR-RAID PRECAUTIONS even involved the city zoos. These men are part of a drill conducted at the Bronx Zoo on April 13, 1942.

chief civilian protection adviser of the Office of Civilian Defense. "They must stay right there and take it, if it comes, up to a certain point." On the back of each seat was a sticker with red and green arrows pointing to the area under the bleachers and grandstands that became makeshift air-raid shelters. The city zoos also got an air-raid plan. At the Bronx Zoo, keepers armed with rifles were instructed to slam cage doors on roaring lions and tigers, chain down elephants, and shoot the poisonous snakes if a bomb fell near the reptile house.

Among New Yorkers who were signing up for the draft were members of the city's police force. In February, a concerned Mayor La Guardia went on his regular Sunday *Talks to the People* radio program on WNYC asking for volunteers to step in and take their place. By the spring, La Guardia had a City Patrol Corps ready and willing to do what was needed. Dressed in GI khaki uniforms, New York City's auxiliary police force pa-

the neighborhood with flashlights and make sure all the houses were perfectly blacked out."

Baseball fans who worried that they would become sitting targets were reassured that the city's three steel-and-concrete baseball stadiums were the safest places for them to be if bombs fell. "The ball players will be the soldiers in that situation," said Harry M. Prince, trolled the Brooklyn waterfront and the ridge of hills on Staten Island, on the lookout for suspicious lights that might be enemy signals. They guarded the mountains of scrap metal collected for the war effort and walked the beaches of Coney Island at night, looking for German spies trying to make a landing. They also became the cop on the beat, keeping the peace as they protected neighborhood kids from bullies and in some cases pursued armed thugs. Members of the corps worked without pay and put in two four-hour shifts every two months in the borough where they lived.

On April 5, as New Yorkers read of another sinking of a U.S. merchant ship by a U-boat off the Atlantic Coast, the city celebrated its

first Easter Sunday during wartime. On the day before, one million New Yorkers wearing General Douglas MacArthur buttons and waving American flags lined upper Fifth Avenue to witness an Army Day Parade, the largest display of the country's military might since 1919 when General John Pershing's troops—fresh from victory after World War I—marched up Fifth Avenue. The city had to have been experiencing a peculiar form of gridlock, because this was the day the

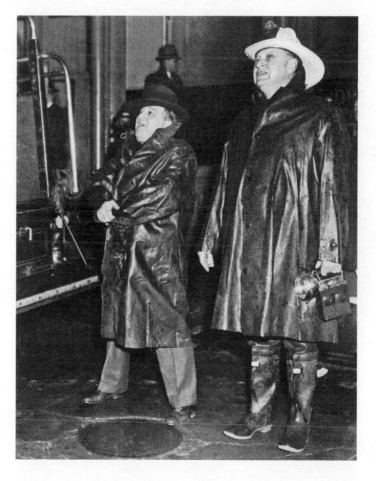

MAYOR LA GUARDIA'S HANDS-on approach to running his city was very reassuring during the war years. Here he is in fireman's garb, witnessing a fire being extinguished in a five-story building on Hudson Street.

SAKS FIFTH AVENUE
had a bond booth on the main floor.
As part of one bond drive the store gave away tickets to Alfred
Hitchcock's *Spellbound*, which starred Ingrid Bergman and Gregory Peck.

circus came to town, with camels and elephants making their way south from the Bronx's Mott Haven railroad yards to Fifth Avenue, which they crossed at 49th Street on their way to Madison Square Garden on Eighth Avenue between 49th and 50th streets.

As Easter Sunday dawned gray and misty, Mayor La Guardia and his wife joined nearly two thousand worshipers on the Central Park Mall to celebrate sunrise services. Another 7,200 gathered inside Radio City Music Hall. In Rockefeller Center's Lower Plaza, beneath the thirty-three flags of the free nations, the center's choristers sang traditional Easter music. There were services on the Upper East Side in Carl Schurz Park and in the Bronx's Pelham Bay Park. The lawn at Sailors Snug Harbor on Staten Island and the West Side Club Tennis Stadium in Forest Hills, Queens, were used for services. So was Brooklyn's Albee Theatre. At Fort Hamilton, where war plant workers just ending their shifts had gathered, they were joined in prayer by servicemen and servicewomen. Later in the morning, New Yorkers filed into St. Patrick's Cathedral, St. John the Divine, St. Bartholomew's, and every church in the city. In the early afternoon, crowds gathered along Fifth Avenue for the largest Easter Parade in the city in twenty years.

By mid-afternoon, police estimated the number at half a million.

They were all here for a war that had not yet been given an official name. On April 3, President Roosevelt held a press conference and appealed to the public to come up with a name for this war. "War with the Axis Powers" was turned down, as was the "Survival War," the president's favorite. "War of World Freedom" was a popular choice, followed by "War of Liberty." Isolationists had a field day, coming up with "The Meddler's War," "Roosevelt's War," and the "War of Imperialism." Ironically, Roosevelt liked neither "World War II" nor the "Second World War," the two names that would eventually stick.

NEW YORK CITY department stores, including Oppenheim Collins on 34th Street, joined in the effort to sell war bonds. Note the models wearing clothing adapted for war use.

"BUY WAR BONDS" SIGNS were everywhere, including on the side of this building on Fifth Avenue.

With each passing month, signs of patriotism in New York City grew stronger. Special cream-colored flags began appearing in the windows of more homes as sons and husbands, and sometimes daughters, enlisted or were drafted into the war. For each member of the family in the armed services, the flags bore a blue star. "My mother put one up in the window for my brother who was in the army," says Doris Lipetz. "We lived in Brownsville, a sweet Brooklyn community, and almost every window had a flag." Flags with gold stars signified the loss of a son or daughter in the war. "There was an almost primitive fear of the telegraph boy coming to the door," says Manny Soshensky, who lived on Manhattan's Sutton Place. What men and women all over New York did want were the boutonnieres and Victory corsages fashioned by Mrs. Douglas Gibbons, a volunteer at the New York War Savings headquarters in Rockefeller Center, who made her patriotic creations out of war stamps. Within a ten-day period over fourteen thousand New Yorkers were sporting the stamp creations, bound in red, white, and blue ribbons and wrapped in cellophane.

Along Fifth Avenue, Bonwit Teller and Saks were two of the department stores that launched defense stamp drives. On Saks's main floor, the red, white, and blue booth became a familiar reminder of the city's ongoing war effort. By the end of 1942, Saks had held a war bond jamboree on its fifth floor, raising $525,000 in under two hours. One $10,000 bond was sold in exchange for getting Hildegarde, the well-known cabaret performer, to sing "The Last Time I Saw Paris." Macy's war bond drives became so ambitious, beginning when thousands of New Yorkers crowded the store's Victory Booth in January 1942, that by July 1944, when their "Bondadiers" sold $3 million worth of "E" bonds in one month, a celebration was in order. Macy's rented Madison Square Garden, where their patriotic employees were entertained by Harry James and his orchestra playing "Two O'Clock Jump."

In May, the Office of War Information launched "The Nature of the Enemy," a dramatic exhibit in Rockefeller Center's Channel Promenade, appropriately placed between the British Empire Building and La Maison Française, and aimed at stirring American blood. The exhibit featured huge installations depicting a shuttered church, a group of gun-toting children in gas masks, and a vivid image of a concentration camp, all disturbing illustrations of life under Hitler. Accompanying the exhibit was a 4,000-pound bomb, the largest ever made in America, on whose surface war bond buyers were invited to scrawl their names.

In early June a massive war bond drive was held in the city. A small army of "Minute Men"—volunteers for the bond drive—began a house-to-house canvassing campaign with the goal of amassing $190 million in pledges. Spreading out into every borough, the volunteers visited 200,000 homes, announcing themselves with the "V" for Victory theme—three dots and a dash—simulating the opening of Beethoven's Fifth Symphony.

Then, on June 13, an unseasonably hot Saturday morning, New Yorkers lined Fifth Avenue from Washington Square to 79th Street for one of the most massive demonstration of patriotism in the city's history. It was called the "New York at War Parade," and nothing was spared to bring home to New Yorkers the need to defend the country against

THIS FOUR-THOUSAND-pound bomb was hauled into Rockefeller Center where bond buyers got the chance to write their names across its surface. Bond buyers were assured that the bomb would fall on enemy territory.

THE U.S. ARMY BAND CROSSING Fifth Avenue after participating in Rockefeller Center's opening ceremony for its Four Freedoms War Bond Drive.

THIS EMOTIONAL display of concentration camp victims was part of Rockefeller Center's "The Nature of the Enemy" exhibit, which ran from May through July 1943.

AS PART OF Rockefeller Center's "The Nature of the Enemy" exhibit, this display of rifle-toting children in gas masks was meant to show the brutal militarization of Germany's youth.

THE "NEW YORK AT WAR PARADE" began downtown at Washington Square and went uptown along Fifth Avenue to 79th Street. A squadron of soldiers has just marched past the Flatiron Building on 23rd Street.

the horrors of Nazi Germany and Imperial Japan. Even the two-block-long reviewing stand in front of the New York Public Library was built to resemble a battleship with a giant "V" across its prow. "It is the duty of every person to participate in New York City's demonstration of its grim determination to do the utmost in helping defeat Hitler and

his Axis partners," announced Mayor La Guardia. And turn out they did, some two million of them, as three hundred stunning floats passed by. One carried a graphic depiction of the horrors Hitler had already inflicted on civilization. Another bore a giant bust of President Roosevelt. Dorothy Koppelman was part of a group of young painters hired to work on the floats: "It was absolutely marvelous. They were majestic. We worked all day on them and slept at night in a settlement house. We built the floats and marched. The parade was tremendous."

The Army, the Navy, and the Marines marched. So did war plant workers and air-raid wardens. Norwegians, Russians, and Greeks marched, along with a delegation of the nations of the Western Hemisphere. Flags waved from office building windows and a blizzard of paper kept raining down, and as the Army strode past the reviewing stand, forty combat planes—including a salvaged German Messerschmitt shot down by the R.A.F.

during World War I—soared across the Manhattan skies.

It took eleven hours for every float and every marcher to pass the reviewing stand. Darkness had fallen by the time the torchlight procession, symbolizing the nation's hopes for peace, turned off 79th Street, where the parade ended. The *New York Times* called the parade "the greatest spectacle of its kind New York has ever seen." John Dowling, an R.A.F. airman who had arrived from Blitz-scarred London, could not control his emotions as he told a *Times* reporter, "I've never seen anything like it. If I was never confident before, I am now. We can't lose."

NOTHING WAS OVERLOOKED during the city's scrap metal drive. Here, workers remove one of four 100-pound cornices on the roof of the Ansonia Hotel at Broadway and 73rd Street. Thousands of pounds of metal would be gathered from the hotel roof's ornamentation.

Rationing for Victory

New York fought the good war. People were working toward a
common goal. It was a wonderful time. Every day was an adventure.

Norman Corwin
Writer, producer, *This Is War!*

New Yorkers listening to radio station WOR in
September 1941, three months before war was declared, heard the
voice of radio personality Joe Ripley speaking to them from Times
Square. He was hosting a program called *Aluminum for Defense*, a
lighthearted response to the country's seven-day aluminum drive.
With the help of some well-known New Yorkers, Ripley was taking the listener on an imaginary "metal" march through the city. In
the background, clanging pots and pans helped deliver the message.
Bill Robinson put himself in the neighborhood he knew best: "Oh,
brother, Harlem is hittin' on all six cylinders. Every time I make

WOMEN ARE WORKING the victory garden on the lawn of the Charles Schwab house. The shuttered palatial mansion, off Riverside Drive between 73rd and 74th streets, had been briefly considered for the official mayor's residence until La Guardia balked at its opulence.

a stop, they're throwin' pans and pots out of the window." Kitty Carlisle hosted her own make-believe aluminum-collection party at the Stork Club, where debutante Josette Daly contributed "gobs of bracelets and hair curlers."

Although New Yorkers were as eager as the rest of the country to do what they could for the war effort—even before Pearl Harbor—they would soon discover that the tin cans used to package their fruits and vegetables were growing scarce. Once America became involved in the war, those tin cans would become almost non-

existent. Less than a month into the war, the *New Yorker* posed the dilemma in its "Talk of the Town" column: "We've been trying to adjust our mind to the idea of a civilization without tin. No more canned peas out of season, no more foil around cigarettes, no more beer in cans." While New Yorkers were not about to brew their own bathtub beer, some, like artist Dorothy Koppelman, rolled their own cigarettes. So did photographer Arthur Leipzig after trying an unknown brand: "They were thirteen cents a pack. I bought one. They were terrible!" As for those precious peas, there was another solution, one used during World War I when Bryant Park was turned into a giant war garden. A few days after that *New Yorker* article appeared, the Office of Civil Defense announced the creation of their nationwide Victory Garden Program, which would include not only every homeowner's back forty, but community gardens as well. "On Staten Island a number of our public spaces were given over to families for Victory Gardens, including the playgrounds," says Mary Shalo, who was twenty-two when the war broke out. "We grew beets, carrots, radishes, and lettuce." Former New York City Parks commissioner Henry Stern remembers the playground at PS 153 in Manhattan's Inwood section being converted to a victory garden: "We kids would grow lettuce and every kind of vegetable." Rockefeller Center had its own "farm" on Fifth Avenue. The flower beds in the Channel Gardens between La Maison Française and the British Empire Building now sprouted onions, lettuce, parsley, cabbages, Swiss chard, and broccoli, with four large boxes brought in for sweet corn. Along the rim of the skating rink hundreds of tomato plants grew. The precious produce from these efforts most likely went to needy families. On Riverside Drive, the expansive grounds surrounding the vacant Charles Schwab mansion between 73rd and 74th streets were turned over to the community for a victory garden. At the corner of York Avenue between 64th and

EVEN ROCKEFELLER Center got into the act. Swiss chard, broccoli, carrots, and sweet corn were now growing in the Channel Gardens. Two hundred tomato plants grew in beds along the rim overlooking the Lower Plaza.

65th streets, the Rockefellers turned over some land belonging to their Institute for Medical Research to the Manhattan Garden Club. The ladies began a Children's Garden, and throughout the summer months six hundred city children worked the subdivided plots, eventually harvesting 36,000 radishes, 7,200 bunches of carrots, 10,000 onions, and 9,500 beets. A small cottage on the site was converted into a country store so these new urban farmers could sell what were literally the fruits of their labors. The smallest patches of land in Manhattan were claimed for victory gardens. Children grew vegetables in a park in Kips Bay, in the shadow of the Con Edison smokestacks. School playgrounds in every borough put space aside so schoolchildren could grow their own vegetables.

Those Garden Club ladies lost no time in getting out their own rakes and spades, slipping those garden gloves over their well-manicured fingers and getting to work. By April, Manhattan's City Garden Club had booked all of their scheduled May tours of the victory gardens that their affluent members had

CHILDREN TENDING THEIR VICTORY GARDENS IN a schoolyard on First Avenue between 35th and 36th streets. Con Edison smokestacks can be seen in the background.

planted on their penthouse terraces and in townhouse backyards. On display were the vegetable gardens surrounding the mansions of Mrs. Andrew Carnegie and Mrs. George Whitney. How odd it must have seemed to see tomato and cucumber vines climbing over terrace walls, or rows of beans and radishes sprouting on the postage-stamp plots behind Upper East Side townhouses! By early spring 1942 every patch of available space in the city, from the elegant penthouses and terraces of Fifth and Park avenues to the poorest tenement fire escapes, had boxes filled with budding seedlings. In case Manhattanites wondered whether they had the green thumbs to handle the job, Macy's fifth floor became a "Vegetables for Victory" garden display, with a team of experts ready to take the intimidation out of gardening. The other four boroughs, where land was more available, practically became truck farms. In Brooklyn, families who didn't have their own backyards or front lawns were given small "victory" plots in the Botanical Garden's Oriental Garden. "My only successful crop was radishes," remembers Arthur H. Westing. In Sunnyside and Woodside, vacant lots across from apartment complexes were subdivided, plowed, fertilized, and seeded. And in nearby Jackson Heights, gardening was done on a grander scale. In 1919, the Queensborough Corporation built the country's first upscale suburban garden apartment complex here, eventually offering its wealthy tenants golf courses and tennis courts, along with lots of gardens. During World War I, the corporation gave over its undeveloped lots to the Jackson Heights Garden Club for victory or "war" gardens. Although there was less open space when World War II was declared, the offer still stood, and in March 1942 four large corner lots between 84th and 87th avenues were leased to the Garden Club. The lots were then subdivided and given over to Jackson Heights residents. By June, strawberries, asparagus, and every kind of vegetable except potatoes were sprouting. The Jackson Heights community was a very active one during World War II. In addition to gardening, the women of the community had clocked in 117,000 hours knitting garments for U.S. soldiers and European refugees. So great were the results of their efforts, in 1943 a B-24 bomber was christened *The Spirit of Jackson Heights.*

While victory gardens helped solve the problem of replacing those peas in the vanishing tin cans, there were other staples—butter, meat, flour, and coffee—that required a trip to the store. By the spring of 1942, with more food going to the war effort, Rationing for Victory, the name given to the government's food rationing program, was instituted across the nation. The idea was to make sure the country's limited food supply was evenly distributed and that Americans with deep pockets had no advantage over the rest of the population. Posters went up in every neighborhood grocery store and butcher shop, instructing housewives on the new rules. With coffee, meat, butter, eggs, and eventually sugar, in short supply, ration books were distributed to every family member. Red stamps covered all fresh food while blue stamps could be used for the diminishing canned and rare frozen items. There were coupons for coffee and coupons for meat and butter. To most people, their ration books were more valuable than money. "You had to be very careful with your ration books," says Mimi Leipzig, who was seventeen and growing up near Brooklyn's Prospect Park when the war broke out. "My mother would stand in line with my coupons to buy things for me, which is how she got pneumonia, standing on one of those meat lines." Once more, Macy's rose to the challenge, this time selling baby chicks and rabbits with incubators, cages, and instructions on raising them. What they didn't tell their customers was how to turn those sweet chicks and baby bunnies into Sunday dinner. Stamp swapping became the new enterprise as people traded stamps for items they didn't use for those they needed. Ethel Ursprung's family were not coffee drinkers: "My mother would trade her coffee coupons with people who had meat or butter coupons. It wasn't terrible. We didn't do without."

Sugar was very scarce, especially after the Japanese invasion of Manila cut off all sugar supplies from the Philippines. With the sugar that did manage to come in from the Caribbean going to the war effort, "sugar buying cards" were issued. Having a card, however, was no guarantee that the precious white stuff would be available. By March 1942, New York women were signing up for the YWCA's newest spring course: a "how-to" on preparing meals in the face of the new war restrictions. The *New York Times* ran a weekly food column featuring recipes using foods that were still abundant. Health took a backseat with some recipes, such as the one calling for bacon drippings to be poured over vegetables and wilted lettuce. Because of the way they

> *I grew up on the Lower East Side in my grandfather's building. He was a very well-known rabbi. Attached to the house was a large yard. P.S. 188 asked if they could use the yard for a victory garden and my grandfather agreed. Each class had its own section of the garden where they grew vegetables.*
>
> —NORMA BOCK

cooked, Italian families managed to eat healthfully and not feel terribly deprived. "We had gravy on Sunday with pasta and meatballs," remembers Joan Harris. "During the week we'd have pasta with broccoli, soup and an omelet with vegetables." Some families became very enterprising. Edna Satenstein's always had butter: "My sister was married to a guy named Bernie who worked for Breyer's Ice Cream. Bernie would bring home heavy cream, which we would churn into butter." There was a lot of vanilla and strawberry ice cream, but no chocolate because of the shortage of cocoa beans.

Meat was another commodity that was becoming more precious. Even though Chicago's stockyards were producing record amounts of beef, much of it was being shipped overseas to feed our army and our allies. The meat that was available in butcher shops was not plentiful and it was not choice. Bea Levine stood on those meat lines: "We never got good cuts of meat and the supply was very limited." By

August, rumors of "meatless days" began circulating among New York's restaurants and on October 20, Mayor La Guardia went on radio urging the city's hotels and restaurants to observe "meatless Tuesdays." The mayor gave restaurants some slack, allowing liver, kidneys, tongue, and other organs to be served in place of beef, veal, pork, and lamb. Hardest hit by the mayor's edict were the city's numerous hamburger joints and hot-dog stands.

The city's hotels and restaurants got right into the spirit of things. Cheese pancakes, vegetarian cutlets, and "nut" burgers were some of the strange items now found on menus at the upscale Hotel Astor and Waldorf-Astoria. The Hotel Commodore began "dressing up" their egg and vegetable dishes with garnishes, hoping that presentation would somehow distract from that missing lamb chop. Rockefeller Center's Rainbow Room and Rainbow Grill were closed indefinitely a few days before Christmas in 1942 because of a shortage of manpower. But its Down Under Room remained open. The Down Under was near the skating rink, where those tomato vines were growing. The kitchen staff got very creative when they concocted their own "cheese-less" version of the classic macaroni-and-cheese dish by substituting chicken and turkey for rationed cheese. At the exclusive Colony restaurant, where customers were accustomed to elaborately prepared dishes, Chef Cavallero could offer nothing to show for his talents but a mundane-sounding celery cheese appetizer and a noodle dish dotted with fresh tomatoes. Nevertheless, in a city that wanted to do its part, customers remained loyal to their favorite eateries.

In the 1940s, New York City's restaurant chains were as much a part of the cityscape as Broadway shows. The ability to get a tasty, dependable meal without breaking the bank had become a birthright in this town, and the most popular chain was the Horn & Hardart Automats, located in every Manhattan neighborhood. Child's and Bickford's cafeterias were in the city too, although not nearly as many. Even with a war on, New Yorkers expected their favorite eating spots to rise to the occasion, and somehow they didn't disappoint. Longchamps and Schrafft's—the two high-end chains—offered dishes like oxtail ragout casserols, deviled fresh lobster, and a chickenless vegetable à la king. Child's served boiled tongue with buttered cabbage, and in a genuflection to the mayor's Italian heritage, it offered *pasta e faggioli*, a filling pasta and kidney beans dish. Both the Automat and Bickford's took advantage of the availability of animal innards. Horn & Hardart's commissary on Eleventh Avenue and 50th Street created a tripe Creole and kidney stew, while Bickford's introduced sautéed kidneys. More challenged were the city's famous steakhouses, such as Keens Chop House on West 36th Street and Cavanagh's on West 23rd Street, where Diamond Jim Brady once dined on thick, juicy slabs of prime rib. Their customers had to forget about those famous chops and steaks, and allow themselves to be consoled with lobster, chicken, capon, and turkey.

As the war dragged on and more men were going overseas, meat grew even scarcer. In January 1945, Mayor La Guardia went on the air again, this time not requesting but ordering restaurants to observe meatless days. And there would now be not one but two days when New Yorkers could not purchase meat. The mayor chose Fridays as the second meatless day, perhaps figuring that at least for the city's large Catholic population, this would not be a hardship. Inevitably, a black market surfaced, with some bank accounts growing fat from the privations of the war. "A lot of people in the produce business did very well, something they won't admit to," said David Diamant, a financial consultant whose father owned a butcher shop on 116th Street and Lenox Avenue. "During the war he was making $500 a week when most people made only $40 or $50. He was able to buy himself a car."

That car probably didn't put many miles on its odometer now that gas was heavily rationed. When the Japanese seized the rubber plantations of the Dutch East Indies, 90 percent of America's rubber supply was cut off, effectively grinding the manufacture of tires to a near-halt. The remaining stock had to be conserved, and since the best way to conserve tires was not to drive on them, the U.S. government decided to ration gasoline. On May 15, 1942, car-driving New Yorkers lined up at local schools to get their official stickers. "A" stickers went to "Sunday" drivers, "B" stickers were given to those whose vehicles were deemed essential to the war effort, and "C" stickers were reserved for doctors, ministers, mail carriers, and railroad workers. Taxis could be driven only six days a week. To make sure drivers didn't cheat, the day of the week on which they were forbidden to drive was stenciled on their cab windows. Even with the 35-miles-per-hour speed limit, supplies of gas were spotty and by June, "Out of Gas" signs posted on filling stations were a common sight.

Although truck drivers got their own "T" stickers, in what was probably a publicity stunt, the Grand Union in Forest Hills, Queens, began using a horse and wagon to deliver groceries. That experiment quickly ended when the grocery chain realized that it was easier to buy horses and wagons than it was to train a

RUBBER COLLECTED by the U.S. Rubber Company was placed into bins that were kept in an underground entrance to Rockefeller Center's RCA Building.

city kid to control a horse. There was one upside to the gasoline shortage. By 1943, the lack of gas at the pumps became a boon to Manhattan's real-estate market. Not only were some suburbanites giving up their houses for city apartments and their cars for the subway, those already living in the city saw no reason to leave.

For New Yorkers living and working in Manhattan there was another perk: with few cars on the streets, the city became a pedestrian's paradise. "My mother worked as a messenger on Wall Street," says Beverly McDermott. "She loved to window shop during her lunch hour, and it was such a pleasure for her to get around town without worrying about traffic." On weekdays, Fifth and Madison avenues had what amounted to Sunday traffic and the side streets were nearly empty. Photographer Arthur Leipzig, who used a car when he shot stories for the newspaper *PM*, was struck by how few cars were on the street: "You could find a parking space anywhere!"

Restricting the use of cars would not be enough to get those vital rubber supplies needed for the Army's guns and shells. Six months into the war, in June 1942, President Roosevelt ordered his intensive sixteen-day "Salvage for Victory" war drive. Scrap rubber was what the president wanted, in every shape and form. Automobile tires, old bathing caps, run-down rubber soles, boots, garden hoses, rubber stamps, syringes, ice bags, garters, and suspenders were on the list of items to be collected and brought to the city's six thousand gas stations. Bergdorf-Goodman and Saks Fifth Avenue were two of the Fifth Avenue department stores that contributed unsold corsets. Saks also put together six window displays featuring "salvage sculptures," including an American eagle and a replica of Uncle Sam made from tin cans and rubber. Macy's deflated its Thanksgiving Day balloons and turned them into 650 pounds of scrap rubber. One of the largest rubber donations came from Horn & Hardart, with five and a half tons of rubber and metal parts given over to the scrap pile. The "21" Club donated its rubber doormat, and Joe DiMaggio threw in his baby's rubber pants. In the subway entrance to Rockefeller Center's RCA Building, the U.S. Rubber Company installed rubber bins for employees with donations. A penny a pound is what the government offered when people brought in their items.

In an effort to conserve gasoline while they gathered up rubber, the Madison Square Boys Club hitched a horse to a wagon and went from street to street, carting the neighborhood rubber scrap to its headquarters at 301 East 29th Street. Wealthy New Yorkers pitched in with the rest of the city. The Pinehurst Garage at 70th Street and Park Avenue gathered five hundred pounds of rubber items from the residents of the nearby apartment houses. Junk dealers and factories quickly offered to help, delivering as much as four thousand pounds of rubber to the gas station owners, whose job it was to weigh the scrap and pay the penny a pound to those who brought it in. They, in turn, would be reimbursed by the government.

In Brooklyn, Bob Lyons, who owned a gas station on Dwight Street, propped a sign on a pile of old tires, and very soon neighborhood kids were scavenging local garages for old tires and vacant lots for

BOY SCOUTS OF
Troop #121 push an old Ford
jalopy into the Westchester Auto Wrecking Company yard at
1400 Blondell Avenue in the Bronx as part of the city's scrap metal drive.

tossed-away shoes. By the time the drive was into its fourth day, the Atlas Service Station on Queens Boulevard had a pile of rubber scrap measuring three feet high and ten feet long. These gas station owners got no money for their efforts, and were responsible for weighing what came in and advancing the money the government promised to pay for the scrap. Still, most of them would go the extra mile, sometimes losing money on the drive, because they knew their efforts were needed.

If New Yorkers thought those piles of rubber tires were impressive, they had no idea what was about to be asked of them. On September 17, Mayor La Guardia launched a drive for scrap metal that was like nothing the City of New York could have imagined. His announcement to the citizens of his city set the tone: "One of the best ways to fight this war is to give the boys at the front weapons and ammunition with which to fight, and the best way to give them weapons and ammunition is to give them the metals from which these can be made." Taking a page from King Herod, the mayor issued a "proclamation" to all five boroughs, as-

signing each one a date when their salvage was due. All the city newspapers were on board, promising to keep their readers up to date on what was expected of them. A single ton of scrap would become two tons of steel for battleships, tanks, and guns, New Yorkers were reminded as they lugged old metal beds and bedsprings from attics, pulled huge metal signs down from vacant stores, and heaved old safes, filing cabinets, and cash registers out from storerooms and brought them to salvage depots. Piles became mounds and mounds became mountains as homes, stores, offices, and warehouses were emptied of every nonessential sliver of metal. People dropped keys—thousands of them—to long-forgotten locks in paper containers placed by the paper industry in stores and theaters throughout the metropolitan area. Cemeteries were not off-limits, as owners were urged to give up the heavy metal chains and bronze posts surrounding their family plots. Neither was the old Tombs prison on 100 Centre Street, as its highly prized "hacksaw-resistant" cell bars were removed and carted away.

The city's history took a backseat as metal feeders and water troughs from the time when fire trucks were horse-drawn went into the scrap pile. So did the cannon carriages and cannonballs dating from the Civil War that guarded Brooklyn's Fort

THESE NEW YORK CITY BOYS ORGANIZED their own tin club, processing in one day more than half the needed tin to build a fighter plane.

PEOPLE STOP TO LOOK AT THE GROWING pile of pots and pans in Times Square, all part of the city's aluminum drive.

THESE STUDENTS AT HARRISON TECHNICAL High School collected nearly thirty thousand pounds of paper, averaging ninety-two pounds per student.

Jay. The Twelfth Regiment threw in a ton of war trophies taken from the Germans in the last war. Con Edison's "Edison Man," a quarter-ton brass, copper, and aluminum sculpture that was part of the "City of Light" exhibit at the 1939 World's Fair, was sacrificed. So were a couple of stoves from the kitchen of President Roosevelt's former townhouses on East 65th Street. Westsiders glancing up at the roof of the Hotel Ansonia on Broadway and 72nd Street would have been struck by the sight of workmen stripping it of its ornate metal cornices. Sentiment had no place in this massive drive. The Brooks Costume Company parted with several suits of armor used in the Broadway production of *The Vagabond King*, and Ray Bolger, who was starring in the Broadway play *By Jupiter*, donated an iron theater counter-weight. And when Samuel Block, an investigator with the Department of Welfare, gave up a vase made from the first shell fired by the Turks against the British in the siege of Palestine, he said, "This shell was originally made in the Krupp works and furnished by Germany to her former ally. I want it to go back to Germany."

As the mountains of metal continued to grow in all five boroughs, Parks Commissioner Robert Moses, who had been put in charge of industrial scrap, had his eye on much bigger stuff. "We have over 9,000 vacant old-law tenements, most of them useless and a menace," Moses said, jump-starting the yet unknown practice that would come to be known as "urban renewal." Moses also had his eye on larger unoccupied buildings like the twenty-two-story Hudson Towers on the corner of West End Avenue and 72nd Street. Everything was scrutinized. Pulling up Brooklyn's nearly three thousand tons of abandoned trolley tracks and dismantling the four steel structures that served as storage yards for old wooden elevated cars made sense. Even stripping the old Aquarium—the circular structure that was once Castle Garden—of its metal was okay, since the structure was being threatened with demolition to make way for the Brooklyn Battery Tunnel. (In a last-minute effort, the historic edifice was saved.) But taking down the subway kiosks or razing the Third Avenue el was not something the city was willing to consider. (Both the kiosks and the el would survive until the 1950s.) In a note of irony, when Manhattan's Sixth Avenue el was taken down in 1938, the same mayor who was now denouncing those who didn't give their all to the scrap drive as "Jap lovers" sold the elevated's metal to Japan.

Enormous mountains of cast-off metal were everywhere. In Manhattan, one rose on Fifth Avenue in front of

St. Patrick's Cathedral, another at the tip of the island, and a third one on 63rd Street between Amsterdam and West End avenues. Rockefeller Center collected one million pounds of scrap gathered from its fourteen buildings. Everything from thumbtacks to a five-ton proscenium arch and a hundred-foot aluminum curtain went into the pile. The old World's Fair parking lot in Flushing Queens was one big scrap heap. At Ebbets Field in Brooklyn, the scrap pile grew rapidly once kids were given free admission if they brought in ten pounds of salvage. Giant's Stadium followed suit. "The New York Giants let kids into the ballgame if you brought scrap metal into the ballpark," says Rocky Doino. "A bunch of us kids would go to an abandoned building and remove the metal weights from windows." Taking a cue from baseball, over one thousand movie theaters, including the Loews Ziegfeld in Brooklyn, held "Salvage Matinees." Anyone bringing in a large piece of scrap metal was given free admission. Nine-year-old Phillip Curtin took part in the drives in Woodside, Queens: "We'd gather the foil from used cigarette packs and roll it into a huge ball. Then we'd take it to the Bliss Theatre where they had a huge dumpster outside. If we brought a certain amount we'd get into the movie for free."

The city's patriotic spirit took a few unusual turns. In Manhattan, the wife of a movie magnate threw two Rolls-Royces and a Hispano-Suiza automobile into the heap. In Brooklyn, Nicklis Constantine, a 56-year-old tavern owner, drove his car into a scrap pile and left it there. Remembering his sixteen nephews who served in the Greek army only to see his native country enslaved, Nicklis said, "I want to give my car for the fight to make all nations free."

At the beginning of Mayor La Guardia's month-long drive, a scoreboard was erected in Times Square sparking a spirit of competition among the five boroughs. Neighborhood vied with neighborhood and in a note of irony, one of the biggest scrap piles in Manhattan was in Yorkville. In an effort, perhaps, to purge its former image, the place where swastikas were once as common a sight as the American flag was now had more effigies of Hitler hanging from their lampposts than in any other neighborhood.

Collecting salvage didn't end with La Guardia's marathon scrap-metal drive. Throughout the war years, New Yorkers continued to do their share. Children collected old newspapers in wheelbarrows and brought them to recycling centers. "We saved paper, we saved scrap metal, we saved everything," says Henry Stern, who collected newspapers and carted them to school in a wagon. New Yorkers who parted with their old cans knew that their efforts yielded enough tin to supply the army with 2,500 tanks or 77,000 fighter planes. The bacon grease inside the cans that housewives brought to their butchers was used to make ammunition. And the nylon stockings that young women donated would eventually become powder bags for naval guns.

Even wreckage from torpedoed ships became part of the city's salvage effort. Residents of Coney Island, Brighton Beach, and all of the communities along the Jersey shore would routinely comb the beaches for parts of lifeboats, instruments, fighting gear, and even food rations that drifted ashore from torpedoed ships and disabled U-boats and turn over what they had found to the naval authorities. And in a grand symbolic gesture of patriotism, the Wrigley Company dismantled its famous ten-foot-high Wrigley Spearmint electric sign that had been darkened since the beginning of the dim-out and had the metal carted off to defense factories. The space it had occupied was donated to the war effort to promote the sale of War Savings stamps.

DURING THE WAR, ROCKEFELLER CENTER'S MALE guides were replaced by women who were dubbed "Centerettes." Here, male guide Stephen Bloyer gives last-minute instructions to a group of female recruits before exchanging his guide cap for one from the U.S. Navy.

New York City's Riveting Rosies

My mother was a messenger for a Wall Street firm. She delivered stocks and bonds. She loved her work. She would get all dressed up in a suit, high heels, gloves, and a hat to go to work. She spent her lunch hour in St. Patrick's Cathedral, saying a novena for the safe return of her son who was fighting in the Pacific.

Beverly McDermott

Women were everywhere. You'd see them operating elevators in office buildings. They were page "girls" or "Centerettes" at Rockefeller Center and bus "girls" at the Waldorf-Astoria. At Pennsylvania Station and Grand Central Terminal their voices announced train arrivals and departures. They sold you railroad tickets at ticket counters and took those tickets from you on the trains. At La Guardia Field they were part of the police patrol, controlling pedestrian traffic and watching for suspicious packages. They flew planes for the Civil Air Patrol. They drove trucks and taxis, tended bar and operated elevators, and in the summer months

BEFORE THE WAR, it was unheard of to see a woman mixing drinks behind a bar. By war's end it was a common sight.

Articles appeared in newspapers praising their efforts and cheering them on.

As men streamed into Pennsylvania Station and Grand Central Terminal on their way to training camps, they left behind not only the service jobs that were vital to keeping New York City running, but the jobs that were helping to support the massive war industry. A year before America's entry into the war, Grumman Aircraft on Long Island was in full production with the Wildcat, a plane that would be critical in the Philippines and the Battle of the Atlantic. They had begun work on the Sto-Wing, a plane with folded wings designed for aircraft carriers. Then came the attack on Pearl Harbor. The aircraft company jumped into wartime mode, scheduling two daily ten-hour shifts with a push for a seven-day workweek, despite the Labor Department's laws requiring one day of rest.

Husbands were off to war, their wives and children needed an extra paycheck, and war plants like Grumman in Bethpage and Republic in Farmingdale needed you'd find them perched atop lifeguard chairs at the city's beaches. Women delivered mail, answered emergency calls at local police stations, and helped run the subways, buses, and trolleys. They were messengers, milkmen . . . sorry, milkwomen, and machinists—riveting, welding, and working the assembly line in war plants and in the Brooklyn Navy Yard.

workers to get their weapons made. Women discovered they could not only bring home a bigger paycheck working for Uncle Sam, they would be doing their bit for the war effort. Twenty-year-old Josephine Rachiele was working in a coat factory when war broke out: "I decided I had to help my country, so I quit my job that Friday and went to Republic." Connie Mancuso, who had five brothers in the armed forces, says, "I wanted to join but I knew that was enough to give my mother a heart attack. I wanted to do something for my country, so I became a riveter." Sophie Sarro also had five brothers in the service and four sisters at home: "My sisters and I all decided to take jobs to help the war effort. We all felt it was the patriotic thing to do." Connie, Sophie, and her sisters all took jobs at Grumman. Connie was a riveter and Sophie worked the assembly line.

It wasn't just airplane manufacturers that needed women's services. The war depended on precision instruments, parachutes, shortwave radios, uniforms, weapons, and even food packagers to assemble the ration kits that kept the army fed. Sylvia Buscaglia sewed parachutes in a Manhattan factory, then switched to soldering in another factory when she found sewing too tedious. Eighteen-year-old Evelyn Margulies drove a tractor for the Army: "I tried to get a job with Sperry Gyro-scope—they had just opened a plant in Fresh Meadows—and the woman interviewing me told me straight out they were not hiring Jews." It seemed that even a war with a common enemy did not eradicate the blatant anti-Semitism that existed in the city. "I was furious," says Margulies. "Then I saw this army poster and I signed up. We worked on the piers in Bay Ridge, loading ammunition."

Not far from the Army's Port of Embarkation was the Brooklyn Navy Yard, the 219-acre shipyard at the edge of the East River nestled between the Williamsburg and Manhattan bridges. The Navy Yard would not only build battleships and aircraft carriers for the war, it would now be the free world's naval repair shop, patching up more than five thousand bombed and torpedoed ships before the war was over. At the height of the war, 75,000 workers would show up for work each day, including budding playwright Arthur Miller, who used his experiences at his job on the night shift as the genesis for *Focus*, his novel on anti-Semitism in America. But now, many of those workers would be women. Newly married Mimi Leipzig began working there right after Pearl Harbor and was given a job as a shipfitter's helper. She says, "We built landing craft. I did tak-welding and I helped measure." Her first day on the job was an eye opener: "We walked into

WOMEN WORKING ON AIRCRAFT WERE OFTEN ASSETS because their small frames allowed them to get into places where men's larger bodies couldn't fit. Here, a group of women are assembling one of Grumman's Avengers.

this room. It was the first tour they gave us and I heard all these jackhammers. I thought to myself, *Well, that will be over soon.* Little did I know that was the sound of the Navy Yard!"

In peacetime it wasn't unusual to see women showing up for work at the Yard, headed for the flag loft, an area set aside for the sewing of flags, streamers, emblems, and bunting. With the war on, the loft maintained a twenty-four-hour, seven-day work schedule. But women were now also performing all the jobs that men had done. Sidonia Levine, whose husband was in the service, put in ten-hour days, six days a week in the Yard, making templates from blueprints of ship sections: "They were wood and we worked on the floor. We were dirty all the time." Hired as a mechanic's helper, she worked with a number of women under a single male mechanic. Working in this man's world had its challenges, as Mimi Leipzig discovered: "We had bathrooms that were only for men. We had the signs changed for women but we couldn't change the plumbing. We always told the new girls the urinals were foot showers."

Some men found it unsettling to suddenly be working among women. "Whenever one of the men dropped a crate he would curse. They were warned about this now that they were working with women," remembers Evelyn Margulies.

Georgette Feller, who was part of the first group of women hired at Republic Aviation as riveters, came up against male resentment very quickly: "I was in final assembly of the P-47 when my supervisor introduces me to a young man and tells him I'm to be his new partner. With that he put down his rivet gun and announced, 'I'm not working with any dizzy broad.' Once he saw that I knew what I was doing we became best of friends. We even dated a few times." It was a little different at the Brooklyn Navy Yard. "Because women usually had traditional jobs, the men there had the feeling we were loose girls," said Mimi Leipzig. Sweaters were suddenly banned from factories and war plants. The reason given was that they could get hooked on the machinery and were therefore a safety hazard. They might have been a hazard, but safety concerns had little to do with it.

For women so accustomed to "female" jobs, the war made their world a whole lot larger. At Grumman Aircraft three young women—Teddy Kenyan, Barbara Jayne, and Elizabeth Hooker—took Hellcat fighter planes and Avenger torpedo bombers for test runs over Long Island's North Shore. While this unlikely trio, each weighing no more than 110 pounds, took the new bombers through their paces in the sky, women on the ground below built and repaired planes. Anne King, a riveter at Republic Aviation, discovered that being a small woman—she weighed just ninety-two pounds—took her into places men could not go: "They were looking for someone who could fit into the air ducts of a new secret jet aircraft they were building. Men could get in but their shoulders were so wide they weren't able to do the work."

Although their paychecks and their horizons were suddenly expanded, working long hours, in rotating shifts, on sometimes physically taxing work was not easy. Two of New York City's Y.W.C.A.s had "swing shift" lounges, where blacked-out rooms were set aside so that women working the late shifts in factories had a place to catch a bite and a bit of shut-eye. Women with young children had it particularly hard. Day-care centers, nannies, and take-out food were not yet a gleam in working women's eyes, and many women had to rely on whatever caregivers were at hand. When they did get home from their shifts, they'd have to shop for food that was not always available because of rationing and then start meals from scratch.

Grumman was one of the plants that had the foresight to realize that an unharried worker was a more efficient worker. They organized car pools and had a Little Green Car service available that would run errands for women workers. If one of them left the gas on at home, the Little

Green Car would be dispatched to her house and someone would turn it off. Two ten-minute breaks were included in every shift and in an effort to cater to female sensibilities, bathrooms were held to a different standard of cleanliness. "They appreciated the fact that we stopped everything in our lives to do this," says Connie Mancuso.

By January 1943 it was apparent to the mayor that if women were to keep working in war plants that demanded rotating shifts, something had to be done to make sure their children were cared for. Public day nurseries were set up in Harlem and Brooklyn, with the other boroughs quickly following. After-school programs were started and special services were provided when women worked the graveyard shift. During summer months play schools opened in settlement houses, churches, and synagogues, private and public schools, community centers, and housing projects.

Women who didn't need the paycheck or who already had jobs became part of an army of civilian volunteers. No sooner had the New Year been rung in than women appeared wherever they were needed. In the second week of January 1942, three hundred women showed up at Police Headquarters at 300 Mulberry Street, where they would learn to do everything from processing applications for air-raid wardens to fingerprinting suspects. Wall Street secretaries did after-hours clerical work for air-raid wardens. And the American Women's Voluntary Services encouraged nonworking women to participate in the citywide child-care program started up by Mayor La Guardia's Committee for the Wartime Care of Children.

As the war continued, more housewives and working women signed up to be airplane spotters. Once a week, Elinore Leo—one of 250 ground observer volunteers from Port Washington—would drop her two children off with a neighbor and climb atop a hundred-foot tower, sometimes braving freezing rain and hundred-mile-an-hour winds, to look for enemy aircraft. Some

SIDONIA LEVINE
(in dark suit) came to work in the
Brooklyn Navy Yard when her husband went to war. Ten-hour days
doing strenuous work was the norm for these women.

THE BROOKLYN NAVY YARD'S FLAG LOFT, where flags, emblems, and bunting were made, was the only area where women were steadily employed. During the war years, the loft was constantly busy.

manned telephone switchboards, ready for the call that told them an unidentified plane had been spotted.

Young women were urged to correspond with servicemen overseas. In a *New York Times* article, writer Cynthia Ozick shared her memories: "Because it was wartime, there was a sense that the country was pulling together. As teenagers, we would write letters to soldiers." Some young women sent the soldiers things from home. Joan Harris sent holy medals to each of her four uncles, hoping the metal would catch any enemy bullets. Mollie Heckerling was twenty-nine and working in a factory when war broke out: "I'd go over to this store on the Lower East Side at the end of the day and help make packages for the servicemen." Women volunteered to check the credentials of servicemen who were routinely given free passes to movies and Broadway shows and at the USO canteens scattered around the city. Mollie was one of them. "Every once in a while I'd go over to Civilian Defense [New York City Defense Recreation Committee] where they'd have some kind of entertainment for the soldiers who came," she says. "It was like a canteen. We'd dance with the servicemen." Republic Aviation had an orchestra and Anne King was its singer: "We'd go to the Hotel Pennsylvania to play. There were loads of soldiers and sailors in the city and I'd dance with them." Contests were held to bring servicemen and young women together for a day of fun in the city. Georgette Feller was one of fifty women selected by her local newspaper for a date with a sailor at Radio City Music Hall. She recalls, "The fleet was in and when we got to Radio City fifty sailors were standing on the grand stairway with numbers in their hands. We got to spend the afternoon with whichever sailor had our number. They gave us a luncheon, then we sat around talking to the boys. After that we saw a movie and the stage show."

Those Rosies in war plants and in the Brooklyn Navy Yard were not only breaking a few molds, they were setting the tone for a very different kind of wardrobe. Skirts, high-heeled shoes, and most jewelry were barred from the Navy Yard, replaced by slacks, coveralls, caps, and turbans so long hair didn't get caught up in the machinery. Sidonia Levine, who liked to eat while she worked, found the blue overalls she wore at the Brooklyn Navy Yard very convenient: "They had millions and millions of pockets, and my mother made little rolls, like butter rolls. Each pocket had a roll in it." "At Republic Aviation we wore shirts and pants," says Georgette Feller. Designer Vera Maxwell was hired by Sperry Gyroscope to design coveralls for the "Sperry girls." In addition to making uniforms for servicemen, Saks Fifth Avenue carried a line of Civilian Defense clothing for women who were air-raid wardens. What seems unremarkable now was very radical in the 1940s, when women wore dresses, hats, and nylon stockings to the grocery store. Josephine Rachiele found the new look unsettling: "I never wore slacks in my life. My sisters and I always wore skirts. It felt weird." "Some women didn't get into it," remembers Georgette, although she liked the look enough to transform part of her husband's uniform after the war into a pair of gabardine slacks.

Like it or not, the war was defining a

PARADES LIKE THIS
one for WAVEs and SPARs on February 8,
1943, were not an uncommon sight during the war years. These 418 young
women were marching to City Hall Plaza, where they would be sworn in to the U.S. Navy and Coast Guard.

new, utilitarian look in fashion. In the first spring since Pearl Harbor, Bonwit Teller featured culottes and slack suits for women bicycling to work or digging their victory gardens, and warm dinner jackets, long-sleeved nightgowns, and fleece-lined slippers for heatless homes. Rogers Peet advertised wool flannel bathrobes for "this year's cooler houses." Bergdorf Goodman themed their clothes to wartime, featuring "Dance for Defense" evening gowns and "Cuddle for Victory" loungewear. Macy's introduced the "Suit Bride," featuring a model wearing a short white veil and a tailored navy suit on the arm of a serviceman. In a move without precedent, to accommodate wartime working women and their hectic "victory schedules" most Fifth Avenue stores, including Arnold Constable, Best & Co., and Bonwit Teller, agreed to stay open until 9:00 on Thursday evenings. Franklin Simon went a step further by introducing speedy fashion service for wartime working women. Everything from lunch to bubble baths and rubdowns, to a room set aside for changing before a festive dinner, were offered to women who were "budgeting time and money on their victory schedule."

With the government's "regulation L-85" restricting the use of fabric to three-and-a-half yards per garment, and with wartime restrictions on wool, rayon, and cotton, the fashion industry had to get very creative. Skirts got shorter, dickeys replaced blouses, and a piece of jewelry had to substitute for now-banned ruffles on collars and cuffs. Designers faced with no metal for zippers or buttons replaced both with bows and stressed durable fabrics that would last for several years. There was no rubber for corsets or garter belts and no nylon for stockings. One enterprising manufacturer came up with a product called "leg-stick," a makeup that substituted for nylon stockings. Women became adept at drawing straight "seams" on the backs of their legs. With corsets, bras, and nylons in increasingly short supply, there was always a run on them whenever women got wind that a new batch was available. The shortage made women easy prey for slippery salesmen. Frances Kelly Vericker remembers the day she got taken: "Somebody was selling nylon stockings on the corner. I raced out and bought a pair and when I got home I discovered there were no feet in them." Raincoats made

from shower curtains, jumpers made from awnings, and outfits fashioned from car upholstery gathered from an automobile graveyard were some of the fashions made from salvage that were exhibited in June 1942 at the Hotel Astor as women demonstrated their ingenuity in the face of shortages. Ironically, the war was providing women, many of whom were earning good paychecks in war plants, with more disposable income than they had ever seen. But with food rationed and clothing restricted to the most utilitarian items, with the exception of movies and live shows, there were few places to spend it.

ON JUNE 11, 1942, a blustery Saturday, New York City held a parade. The war brought lots of parades to the city, but this one was unique. It was an "all-women" parade, the first of its kind. Ten thousand strong, they showed up

THESE NEWLY SWORN-IN WAVES AND SPARs board a special subway that will take them from City Hall Plaza to commissioning ceremonies at Hunter College in the Bronx. All of New York celebrated "WAVEs and SPARs Day" on February 8, 1943.

in crisp uniforms and elegant fur coats. Air-raid wardens and Red Cross workers, members of the Division of War Production Training, Civilian Defense Volunteers, and the American Women's Hospital Reserve Corps all marched down Fifth Avenue from 86th to 62nd Street. Mayor La Guardia was there, joined by thousands of spectators.

The war was changing the face of the city and the roles of the women who lived here. Instead of lunching at Schrafft's, they could now be found staffing booths around town, recruiting WAVEs and WACs. In the wee hours of a Sunday morning, a small group of them were behind their desks at 99 Park Avenue, the headquarters of the Defense Recreation Committee, trying to find hotel rooms for servicemen. Every day at noon, Ann Fehety positioned herself behind a plate-glass window at Pershing Square, recruiting for the Civil Defense Volunteer Organization. Five other women soon joined her, with their eyes on a drive to recruit auxiliary firemen. What they planned was to hop aboard a fire truck and take it through the city streets. When called upon, women could do almost anything. "I worked ten hours a day, seven days a week," remembers Sophie Sarro. "We all wanted to do something to help the war."

SERVICEMEN GET THEIR SHOES SHINED in Duffy Square. Nearby is the Pepsi-Cola canteen, where they could freshen up before using their free passes to one of the Times Square movie houses.

On the Town!
Entertaining the Troops

We would go into the city to these dances at one of the big hotels—the Commodore and the Hotel Pennsylvania—where there were young men in uniform. We'd meet sailors from every country and dance until midnight.

Ethel Ursprung

There were dances all over town. I met lots of girls, very nice girls. There were girls who were in Broadway shows. I dated one of them for a while.

Lieutenant Commander Raymond Langfield

Times Square belonged to the servicemen. During the war years it was the city's gift to the American men and women who were fighting the good fight, and to the soldiers and sailors from England, Scotland, Australia, Canada, and New Zealand, all the free countries whose ships brought them

to New York City. Even with the dim-out darkening the great signs and gas rationing emptying the streets of their honking traffic, even though sidewalk chatter was as soft as the lights in this barely incandescent square, the Great White Way was still a helluva lot of fun. Raymond Langfield, a lieutenant commander in the Navy, came into Manhattan whenever his ship was docked at the Brooklyn Navy Yard for repairs and supplies. He recalls, "The officers had a meeting place in Times Square. It was the bar in the Hotel Victoria." From there, Langfield and his buddies would do the town. "I dated a girl who was in the *Billy Rose Review.* We'd go out after the show, which was around eleven o'clock. Real scotch was scarce, so we'd take a cab downtown to one of those old speakeasies where they actually served liquor in teacups."

The Astor Theatre's marquee may have been dimmed, but up on the hotel's famous Astor Roof, the lights were bright and the music was lively. Laughter and applause still filled the theaters, much of it coming from servicemen who were routinely given free passes. Movies were free too, and on any given night the seats in the Roxy or the Criterion were filled with men and women in uniform. So was Gay Blades, on 54th Street off Eighth Avenue, with a roller-skating rink upstairs and an ice-skating rink below. A soldier or a sailor could dance the night away to the music of Benny Goodman at the Hotel Pennsylvania, Guy Lombardo at the Hotel Taft, or one of the big bands at the Arcadia Ballroom on 52nd Street and Broadway or Roseland, one block south. Lieutenant Commander Sylvan Barnet liked to be close to the heavens: "We'd go to the Starlight Roof of the Waldorf Astoria or the Astor Roof where we'd dance under the stars." Barnet also liked to go down to Greenwich Village, "to Hazel Scott's and El Chico's on Washington Square. They had small orchestras and a whole bunch of booze." Jazz-lover Murray A. Valenstein, who was stationed at Fort Monmouth, would head for the best clubs as soon as he arrived in the city: "I went to Kelly's Stable on Swing Street, where I heard Coleman Hawkins play fifteen choruses of 'Body and Soul' on his sax. That was real sweet." The Stork Club, the Copa, El Morocco, and just about every nightclub put servicemen at the front of the line. Ray Stone, an officer in the city on leave after his ship, the *Intrepid*, had been torpedoed, went to the Stork Club, where he romanced the cigarette girl. "She was a natural beauty with her tray of Camels, Lucky Strikes, and Old Golds," he remembers. "We made a date and I took her to the Commodore, where we danced to Vaughn Monroe. The date ended with a friendly kiss as I put her on the subway to Brooklyn. When I told the guys on the *Intrepid* that I went dancing with a cigarette girl from the Stork Club they were so impressed. You'd have thought I went on a date with Betty Grable." Artist Ray Kintsler, who was stationed at Fort Dix, had his own way of meeting girls: "We'd take our leaves on Wednesday and head for Yorkville because we heard that in that part of town Wednesdays were the maids' night off." Former CBS anchorman Walter Cronkite favored Toots Shors: "I was one of the 'incumbents,' Toots' word for his regulars. I was in the United Press International bureau

You'd see lots of people in uniform. Every bar was crowded. When we came into New York we would have what was called an availability at the Brooklyn Navy Yard for ten days or so. That meant they'd fix up the ship, get the stores loaded, and get it ready to sail again. We didn't want to waste any of that time sleeping.

—LIEUTENANT COMMANDER
RAYMOND LANGFIELD

day and night but on my off time Betsy, my wife, and I got to know Toots pretty well."

Lou Walters's Latin Quarter opened its doors for the first time on April 22, 1942. "Lots of servicemen on leave visited and my father never charged them," remembers ABC's Barbara Walters. Every big hotel had a big band; servicemen were encouraged to swing. There were servicemen's clubs all over town. Officers had a Penthouse Club at the Henry Hudson Hotel and one at the Commodore Hotel, where the staff would find rooms for them. The Green Room at the Hotel Edison made a unique accommodation to servicemen and women. It was called the "2-4-I," which meant that from noon to three, anyone in the service could drop in with a guest and get two lunches for the price of one. Pepsi-Cola had a servicemen's center on 47th Street between Broadway and Seventh Avenue where a guy could catch a shave and a shower and, if he was hungry, a hamburger for a nickel. Members of the venerable Lambs Club provided dinners and

My friend and I would go to these big dances that were held at hotels like the Commodore or the Hotel Pennsylvania in Manhattan. We'd meet soldiers from every country. There was dancing until twelve; then the band would play "Auld Lang Syne" and it would be over.

—ETHEL URSPRUNG

entertainment to servicemen. There was even a "Free France" Canteen in a storefront on Second Avenue between 42nd and 43rd streets. Bill Vericker was there when Marlene Dietrich showed up. He says, "Everyone stood around to hear her sing the national anthem." In November 1942, Frances Hawkins, a secretary at the Museum of Modern Art, sent a heartfelt letter to one of the museum's donors, soliciting funds for afternoon teas:

Men on leave like to sleep late or sightsee. Evenings is theater and movies, also parties. From 4 to 7 there is little to do, and as winter draws on and the afternoons grow dark and cold, many of the men will be homesick and lonely.

Ms. Hawkins was also thinking about the British, Canadian, and Australian soldiers in New York City, whom she felt would be grateful for a place where they could feel a connection to home.

And then there was the Stage Door

SERVICEMEN WERE GIVEN
free passes to all Broadway
shows during the war years.
A group applauds at the St.
James Theatre, where they
are watching a performance
of Rogers and Hammerstein's
Oklahoma!

BROADWAY STARS LIKE ETHEL
Merman would often drop by
the Stage Door Canteen after
a performance to entertain
servicemen.

Canteen. Nestled in the basement of the West Forty-fourth Street Theatre, this brainchild of the American Theatre Wing was open from 5:00 in the afternoon until midnight, and every night of the week soldiers and sailors would line up in front of its red door. The Canteen served free sandwiches and soft drinks, but the real attraction in this intimate space were the

THE MUSEUM OF MODERN ART OPENED its doors to servicemen, providing entertainment in its sculpture garden. Here, accordion player Beulah Berson serenades a group.

HOSTESSES AT THE STAGE Door Canteen were usually showgirls and aspiring actresses. Some of these servicemen may have danced with Angela Lansbury or Lauren Bacall, both of whom were volunteers.

THESE TICKETS entitled servicemen to free sandwiches and non-alcoholic drinks at the Stage Door Canteen.

FOOD CHECK
American Theatre Wing
STAGE DOOR CANTEEN
44904
AMERICAN TICKET CO., BROOKLYN, N. Y.

Broadway stars who were always dropping in, and the Canteen's young hostesses. On any given night Gertrude Lawrence, who was appearing in *Lady in the Dark*, or Alfred Drake, who had just opened in *Oklahoma!*, could be found serving coffee and doughnuts or helping in the kitchen. Most of the hostesses were aspiring actresses and showgirls. Angela Lansbury was a starstruck acting student when she showed up. She said, "I got to see all the great stars there. I danced with the boys. We would jitterbug like crazy. It was the most exciting time of my life." Lauren Bacall was ushering at the St. James Theatre, just down the street. She wrote about it in her autobiography, *By Myself and Then Some*: "The Stage Door Canteen was about to open in New York and it needed hostesses. Only theatre folk qualified. I signed up for Monday nights. I was to dance with any soldier, sailor, or marine who asked me—get drinks or coffee for them, listen to their stories. Many of them had girls at home—were homesick—would transfer their affections to one of us out of loneliness and need."

Robert F. Gallagher was on a weekend pass from his embarkation camp outside

SINGER PEGGY LEE and bandleader Tommy Dorsey were part of the cavalcade of stars that appeared in the film *Stage Door Canteen*.

of the city when he visited the Canteen: "It was a swinging spot that closely resembled a nightclub with a combo or a full-sized orchestra playing great music. The place was crowded with servicemen from all branches, and there were lots of girls." Gallagher dated one of the hostesses: "She fixed up several of my friends with her friends. Those girls showed us a great time, and we really saw the nightlife of New York City." The Stage Door Canteen became so iconic that it was the subject of a novel and a 1943 movie starring Judith Anderson and Tallulah Bankhead. And in his 1942 Broadway show *This Is the Army*, Irving Berlin wrote a valentine to

SERVICEMEN WAITING FOR THEIR TRAINS back to their bases catch some shut-eye on the stairs in Pennsylvania Station's main waiting room.

the place, which he very appropriately titled "I Left My Heart at the Stage Door Canteen."

All of New York City opened its arms to the servicemen who streamed in for their precious few days of leave. Ten-year-old Joan Harris would take the BMT express from Brooklyn with her older sister to Times Square. She says, "When you saw a soldier or a sailor on leave you gave them great respect." Eleven-year-old Edna Satenstein would ride the el from 233rd Street and White Plains Road in the Bronx to Grand Central Terminal: "We'd get off and explore the city. I remember as a little girl it was so exciting to see the soldiers and the sailors. And everybody was so good to them. They'd be on leave. A lot of them would be in Times Square. Sometimes people would just talk to them and tell them how proud they were of them. For servicemen and servicewomen, New York was an exciting place to be."

Most of the servicemen came here by train, arriving in Pennsylvania Station and Grand Central Terminal, and there was not a day during the war years when

THIS SAILOR PASSES THE TIME UNTIL HIS TRAIN arrives in Grand Central Terminal's servicemen's lounge.

those train stations weren't filled with soldiers and sailors arriving or departing. Tom McLaughlin was twelve years old when he stood in Penn Station with his parents and his sister on a Sunday afternoon in late 1942. They were seeing off his Uncle Frank, whom the young McLaughlin idolized. This was the first leg of a journey that would take his uncle to the South Pacific. He remembers: "Looking down on the Concourse floor I saw thousands of brave young servicemen with their families, kissing and hugging and nervously awaiting the opening of the gates leading to the trains. I knew that for some these would be their final good-byes."

To make things easier for these men, there were USOs in both stations, and the Travelers Aid Society operated servicemen's lounges distributing coffee and snacks and food coupons so servicemen who missed their trains could get a meal. There were also billiard tables, writing desks, and a piano. Celebrities taking a train from one of the stations would stop in the lounge and chat with the men and women in uniform. By the spring of 1944, the lounge at Pennsylvania Station would be expanded to accommodate fifty "sleep decks"—deck chairs and blankets—for servicemen in need of some shut-eye before they caught their trains. The station even had a nursery in the women's lounge equipped with cribs and bottle warmers. A nurse was on duty so that infants could be cared for while wives bid their husbands good-bye.

In the summer of 1942, it seemed that all of New York and its outlying beach communities belonged to the Army and the Navy, and no one was complaining. In July, the U.S. Army Air Force took over Atlantic City's Hotel Traymore and its massive Convention Hall. Other major hotels would follow and the seaside resort, with its famous boardwalk now being used for drills and marches, would become known as "Camp Boardwalk." A month later, the U.S. Navy took over a group of hotels in Asbury Park and the exclusive Lido Club, at Lido Beach on Long Island. It also requisitioned the Half Moon Hotel on Coney Island's boardwalk for a convalescent hospital. Manhattan Beach, right next to the amusement park, was taken over by the U.S. Coast Guard and the Merchant Marines. By 1943, servicemen wanting to test the waters off Jones Beach would have their own clubhouse when the Marine Dining Room in the West Bathhouse was given over to the USO.

Baseball tickets were distributed to servicemen for all three ballparks. Any soldier or sailor who was at the Polo Grounds on August 3, 1942, for the "twi-night" game between the New York Giants and

OFFICERS AT THE ARMY BASE ON Governor's Island help their children catch up on homework. The base provided family living quarters and a four-room schoolhouse.

THIS POIGNANT SCENE IN NEW YORK CITY'S PENNSYLVANIA
Station occurred daily as servicemen returning to their bases said
good-bye to their families. The war years stretched the station's
capacity to accommodate travelers. In 1945, one hundred and
nine million passengers occupied Pennsylvania Railroad trains.
The majority of them were servicemen and women.

the Brooklyn Dodgers witnessed something he'd never forget. With the citywide dim-out strictly enforced, the game had to end no later than one hour after sunset. On August 3 that meant 9:10. This particular game was unique: it was being played for the benefit of the Army Emergency Relief Fund, attracting the largest crowd ever to the Polo Grounds. To accommodate the spectators, bullpens were moved forward and, in a precedent-setting accommodation, standees were permitted in deep center field. The atmosphere took on a World Series energy as eager fans filled the stadium seats. The seventh-inning stretch promised to be pretty lively, with Fred Waring's orchestra and 150-member choral group on hand along with the 2nd Corps' Fort Jay band.

At the bottom of the ninth, the Giants were trailing 7–4 when, with two on and no one out, the New York team suddenly rallied. Fans were now on the edge of their seats when, at exactly ten minutes past nine, the switch was pulled and the Dodgers took the game. Booing Giants fans drowned out Fred Waring's national anthem, and frustrated Giants president Horace Stoneham canceled all twi-night games. The exception was the one scheduled for the following night. In that game, the 9:10 Lights Out policy resulted in an equally frustrating ninth-inning tie with the Dodgers.

With gas rationing and wartime work schedules limiting their travel, New Yorkers celebrated the Fourth of July—the first with the country at war—close to home. Railroad stations, bus terminals, and the New York subway were all jammed with New Yorkers trying to get to a patch of sand and a cool ocean breeze. Coney Island had record crowds, and since many of the hotels at Asbury Park and Atlantic City were now being used by the Army, there was not a room to be had on the Jersey shore. The servicemen who decided to spend their holiday in Times Square found themselves sharing the sidewalks with New Yorkers who had given up the ghost of a weekend in the country. Streets usually filled with cars from out of town were now taken over by bicyclists, including women wearing those new slacks and culottes. No fireworks were allowed in the night sky, and the only noise Manhattanites could associate with this holiday were the guns that went off at noon on nearby Governor's Island and the super siren atop the RCA Building, signaling the city's remaining 408 air-raid sirens to test their wails.

Labor Day was a replay of the Fourth, but with even more people on the move. One cop on the beat compared the crowds at Times Square to New Year's Eve, as people jammed the sidewalks or lined up for tickets for Broadway shows or movies. If they were in front of the Criterion Theatre, they could have met Mayor La Guardia and his wife on line, buying tickets for Abbott and Costello's *Pardon My Sarong*. Possibly more than a lack of gasoline or vacation time was at play here. A city that was sharing the pain of this war may have felt the need to find release among its own, and among the soldiers and sailors who would soon be gone.

The year 1942 was one of firsts, and in November, New York City was about to celebrate its first Thanksgiving at war. It would also be the city's first Thanksgiving without a Macy's Thanksgiving Day Parade. New York was not in a festive mood, and since rubber and helium were precious commodities, it wasn't a good idea to use them for anything as frivolous as giant balloons. The holiday was also given its own calendar day by the president. From now on, the fourth Thursday in November would be synonymous with Thanksgiving. It would be the first Thanksgiving that the city played host to every soldier and sailor who could not sit at his family table. A *New York Times* article reflected the mood of the city: "The turkey and the man in uniform will be the most important elements in the celebration of the city's first wartime Thanksgiving in twenty-five years." At the strong insistence of the New York Defense Recreation Com-mittee, that included the WACs and WAVEs.

Even if rationing made the traditional Thanksgiving meal less bountiful, the USO encouraged New Yorkers with room at their tables to invite servicemen to dinner. In homes all over the city, an extra place was set for a young man or woman in the service who couldn't be with family. The city's restaurants and nightclubs opened their doors. The Stage Door Canteen extended its hours and carved up two hundred turkeys for the four thousand servicemen they expected to serve. Another four hundred sailors, soldiers, and marines were treated to Thanksgiving dinner at the Soldiers and Sailors Club on Lexington Avenue. There were Thanksgiving Eve parties and dances all over town like the one the "Steno Canteen" organized, and the dinner and entertainment the Maple Leaf Club on Fifth Avenue held for American and Canadian servicemen. The Museum of Modern Art, which regularly hosted parties for servicemen in the museum's garden, hired Hughie the clown and his three performing dogs to provide entertainment.

The city's hospitality extended itself through Christmas, with more dinners and dances and invitations to the homes of New Yorkers. The Savoy Plaza and the Hotel Edison were two of the city's many hotels that threw parties. In the servicemen's lounges in Pennsylvania Station and Grand Central Terminal, volunteers wrapped Christmas presents. Although the Rockefeller Center Christmas tree would remain unlit until 1945, when the war ended, the Rockefeller Center Choristers sang Christmas carols beneath a trio of Christmas trees.

The city was in a somber mood on December 31, 1942, with German advances in Europe and defeats by the Allies in the Pacific very much on everyone's minds. It seemed fitting that this was the

A VISIT TO THE CENTRAL PARK ZOO WAS ONE WAY for servicemen and women to enjoy the city.

HARLEM WAS A POWDER KEG waiting for a spark, and on August 2, 1943, that spark touched off a riot. Here, women are arrested after looting a store.

first New Year's Eve when the giant white globe did not descend from the Times Tower. The crowd here, many of whom had sons, brothers, and husbands in the war, made do with beams of light from the city's plane-spotter stations crossing the night sky. Meyer Berger, writing for the *New York Times,* described the

young people here as moving "zombie-like through the dimness." Near Duffy Square, a WNYC radio announcer stood in a sound truck and asked for ten seconds of silence to remember servicemen fighting the war, and when Lucy Monroe began to sing the "Star-Spangled Banner" the crowd solemnly joined in. Berger wrote, "War somehow laid its hand on the celebration and tended to mute it."

Through all of 1943, New York City continued to welcome the country's servicemen and women as if they were entertaining the sons and daughters of out-of-town cousins. By summer, news of the Allied landing in Sicily and the possibility that Italy's surrender was just a month or two away was making it easier to laugh. In Times Square, long lines formed outside the Hollywood Theatre to see the screen version of Irving Berlin's *This Is The Army*, featuring Lieutenant Ronald Reagan. When servicemen weren't dropping into the Stage Door Canteen they could be found at the Capitol Theatre, where the movie was drawing large crowds. If they missed *Casablanca*, which opened a few weeks after New Year's Day, they could see *Watch on the Rhine*, Dashiell Hammett's screen adaptation of Lillian Hellman's 1941 anti-Nazi play, now at the Strand, or *The Army Play-by-Play*, a revue written and produced by soldiers that was running for two weeks at the Martin Beck Theatre. The Hotel Sheraton had just opened an "air-cooled" canteen for merchant marines, featuring the entire cast of the Ziegfeld Follies. If servicemen weren't at baseball games, they might be swimming at the Y.W.C.A. under the watchful eye of female lifeguards, or dancing in the Marine Dining Room out at Jones Beach.

Black servicemen didn't have as easy a time of it. You would find them in Times Square and in the jazz clubs on Swing Street, but as a group black servicemen and servicewomen gravitated to Harlem, where they knew they'd be more welcome. If they took in a show at Radio City Music Hall, there were no blacks in the Rockettes line. Policy forbade it on the grounds that a black dancer would be a distraction from the group's uniform look. Four months after Dorie Miller, a black sailor, earned the Navy Cross by downing several Japanese planes at Pearl Harbor, black men lining up at Navy recruiting stations in New York City were being turned away. (Like Miller, the only job a black man could have in the U.S. Navy was working in the ships' mess halls.) Even heavyweight champion Joe Louis, drawing a crowd of seventeen thousand in Madison Square Garden on January 9, 1942, for the Navy Relief Society and donating his $100,000 purse to the victims of Pearl Harbor, couldn't get the Navy to budge. Later that year, the "Brown Bomber" arrived in his chauffeur-driven limousine at New York's Fort Upton, where he would become Private Joe Louis. He would later say of his time there, "They gave me my uniform and sent me over to the colored section." On June 16, 1942, the same day they learned that the U.S. Navy still wasn't prepared to accept their services, 18,000 blacks held a rally in Madison Square Garden, sponsored by the March on Washington Movement for Equal Rights for Negroes, demanding that they be given equal opportunities in the armed forces.

No wonder black men on leave from their segregated military units would rather dance at the Savoy Ballroom on Lenox Avenue than at Roseland. Up on 125th Street, they would take in a show at the Apollo or check out Small's Paradise. Their compensation was some of the best music played by the best musicians in the city. There was also a Servicemen's Center for them on Seventh Avenue at 137th Street, partly paid for by several hundred children of Harlem who wanted to contribute to the war effort.

But Harlem was a pressure cooker just waiting for the heat to become intense enough to blow off its lid. That explosion was ignited on August 2, 1943, a steamy Monday evening in the lobby of the Braddock Hotel at 126th Street and Eighth Avenue, when a white police officer shot a black soldier. Rumors became the match that turned a neighborhood seething with silent rage into a firestorm. Was the soldier killed? Was the woman he was defending at the time of the attack his mother? (The soldier, Private Robert Bandy, had received a flesh wound after struggling with police officer James Collins, whom he believed

to be mistreating a black woman. In fact, Margie Polite was being arrested by Collins—who had been on patrol duty in the seedy hotel—for causing a disturbance.) Before those facts were learned, a shower of glass covered Harlem's streets as white-owned stores from 110th to 145th Street and from Eighth Avenue to Fifth Avenue were smashed and looted. The crowd that had gathered in front of Sydenham Hospital to rescue Bandy—now patched up and escorted out of a back entrance—quickly gathered strength. A ragtag army of Harlem youth claimed the streets, multiplying as the night went on. Armed with bottles and stones, they climbed onto tenement roofs and spread through the stunned neighborhood, carving a path of destruction.

Mayor La Guardia was quick to respond. That first night, he ordered a 10:30 curfew. His City Patrol Corps worked alongside the police department and the Air Warden Service, which included 150 women and a group of deputized black civilians. From his makeshift headquarters in the West 123rd Precinct, where the first alarm had gone out, the mayor gathered the leaders of Harlem. Dr. John H. Johnson, a police chaplain and pastor of nearby St. Mark's Church, arrived at the station. Assistant District Attorney Francis Rivers came, as did William White, secretary of the NAACP. The mayor put

THE AFTERMATH OF
pent-up rage is evidenced in these looted Harlem storefronts.
Unfortunately, in 1943 only the behavior was addressed and not the root causes.

them all on WNYC radio and on police sound trucks, which he dispatched through the streets of Harlem, instructing them to plead with the residents to bring the violence to an end. He even asked Bill "Bo Jangles" Robinson to make an appeal to the crowd.

The orgy of anger lasted two days.

When it was over, five hundred people had been injured, five were dead, and all of Harlem was turned into a gaping wound. "Just a bunch of hoodlums stealing from their own," the mayor would say of the angry young men who wrecked their neighborhood, never addressing the injustice behind the rage. Harlem leaders did come forward with solutions, but they all had to do with equality, a notion with which neither the city nor the nation was ready to grapple. James Baldwin, who was about to turn nineteen when the riots occurred, eloquently put the terrible incident in perspective: "It would have been better to have left the plate glass as it had been and the goods lying in stores. It would have been better but it would have also been intolerable, for Harlem needed something to smash."

As the city tried to heal its wound and get on with the business of life during war, there was good news coming from Europe and from Japan. In his fireside chat on September 8, President Roosevelt announced that Italy had surrendered to the Allies. War in the Mediterranean theater was far from over, but there was no doubt that the Allies had turned a major corner. A month later, on October 26, Emperor Hirohito announced that the situation in his country was grave. Such pessimism on his part could only give the Allied forces fighting in the Pacific cause to rejoice.

It was November 1943, the second Thanksgiving in wartime New York City, and the streets were more crowded than ever. Every hotel room was booked as people continued to arrive in the city's two railroad terminals and its bus depots. Once again, hotel restaurants, private homes, and the Stage Door Canteen opened their doors to servicemen for the traditional Thanksgiving meal, but this year something would likely be missing. With food shortages even more critical, many tables would not have a Thanksgiving turkey to carve. Ham, chicken, duck, even goose could be had, but a traditional tom was not easy to find.

The city remained packed through Christmas with the faces of servicemen everywhere. On Christmas Eve, every church was filled to capacity as prayers were offered for the safe return of sons and brothers and for the end of a war that had already cost so many lives. On Christmas Day, radio station WMCA broadcast a five-hour program via shortwave, allowing New Yorkers to hear the voices of their sons and daughters, boyfriends and husbands, stationed in every part of the world.

A wave of optimism gripped the city as it was about to ring in 1944. With Allied forces gaining ground in Germany and Japan, there was a feeling in the air that an important corner had been turned. Dances were being held everywhere to celebrate the end of 1943 and with it, the possibility that a light could be seen at the end of that long, dark tunnel. The ladies at 99 Park Avenue were very busy handing out invitations for the forty-three organizations affiliated with the New

York City Defense Recreation Committee, who were all giving parties. As servicemen and women kept streaming into the city, sometimes standing in the aisles of trains arriving in Pennsylvania Station and Grand Central Terminal, halls were being booked for dances. Even private apartments were getting ready to throw open their doors for smaller soirees. The Jewish Congress booked Manhattan Center. The Soldiers and Sailors Club opened its doors for a huge celebration. City Center was taken over by the Women's Service Brigade of the International Ladies Garment Workers Union. Kate Smith was appearing at the Stage Door Canteen, and the Steno Canteen was outdoing itself with a gala affair.

And once more, the city gathered itself in Times Square, which gave the best party of all. *New York Times* reporter Meyer Berger was there again among the crowds, who were smiling more broadly and shouting louder than they had the year before: "Times Square crowds moved into the new year last night with the same spirit that moved the Allied world everywhere." To celebrate the new sense of impending victory sweeping the city, dimout rules were relaxed for the first time since the war, and Times Square did not go dark until 10:00 p.m. How long had it been since New Yorkers could take in the theater marquees lit up in their famil-

iar neon? Or see the rows of incandescent lights blazing on the facades of hotels and restaurants? When the lights did go out at 10:00, horns still blew and cowbells clanged and the laughter was louder than ever. So what if the big glass ball that ushered in the new year was still in mothballs? Just give it a year and it would be right back where it belonged, at the top of the Times Tower!

Even in daytime, the war years turned Times Square into a magnet for soldiers and sailors. It also drew teenage girls— some as young as thirteen—who were interested in meeting those soldiers and sailors. With many of their mothers working odd shifts in war plants, girls were left to their own devices, and those devices often led them to Times Square. In February 1944, the New York City Police began to monitor them. Ethel Ursprung, who worked in the city, would meet friends there for dinner and a movie. She recalls, "There was a problem with runaways. Young girls from other parts of the country would come here because they were enamored of service men. I remember they put a curfew in the Times Square area." Acting Captain John J. Cronin, who headed the Missing Persons Bureau at Police Headquarters, formed a "bobby socks brigade," adding eleven policewomen to his staff. Nightly, girls on their own or accompanied by soldiers and sailors were

TIMES SQUARE, THE "CROSSROADS OF THE World," was the perfect setting for war bond drives. Movies like MGM's 1944 *Thirty Seconds Over Tokyo* often provided the kick-off to a drive.

questioned. If their answers aroused suspicion, their names were checked against the list of those reported missing.

The new year brought with it more signs of patriotism, and what better place to display them than in Times Square? A sixty-foot plaster and concrete statue of Lady Liberty sponsored by the Motion Picture War Activities Committee was installed, along with a giant cash register, which served as her pedestal and a reminder of the city's commitment to the war bond drive. Bond buyers got to see their names rung up on the cash register and an extended platform turned Times Square into a huge outdoor theater. Almost daily, show-biz personalities would appear at noon, entertaining the lunchtime crowd. If it wasn't Artie Shaw serenading them with his golden clarinet, impresario Mike Todd would be up there with a string of chorines doing high kicks. On January 17, 1944, the city threw a massive bond rally, and once more that platform became a stage, this time for Jeanette MacDonald, Bill Robinson, Laraine Day, and Jimmy and Tommy Dorsey, who joined fifty war heroes to kick it off.

New York radio station WNEW became a major contributor to the bond drive when Martin Block, the station's well-known disc jockey, began playing a funny song that had been handed to him by a "cute little fellow with a pancake hat." The man was Spike Jones, and the song, "Der Fuhrer's Face." The song was an instant hit and in such high demand that Block decided to play it only after he sold $5,000 worth of war bonds on the air. Block quickly raised the amount to $25,000, and by week's end the disc jockey had sold a quarter of a million dollars' worth of bonds and given a jump-start to Spike Jones's career.

Patriotism was now part of every New Yorker's daily life. In May, Mayor La Guardia unveiled a Times Square billboard promoting the upcoming "I Am an American Day" in Central Park. The following month, when summer came to the city, Central Park was the setting for the first of a series of "Starlight Dances" held in the Heckscher Pavilion. As a fourteen-piece Navy band played, salesgirls from Gimbels and Macy's and secretaries from the city's office buildings danced with soldiers and sailors under the moonlight. On August 23, at 5:00 in the afternoon, some of those soldiers and sailors were likely

part of a crowd that had gathered at Rockefeller Center, filling every available space as Metropolitan Opera singer Lily Pons took her place below the statue of Prometheus in the center's Lower Plaza. As confetti rained down

AFTER A LONG NIGHT ON THE TOWN, a soldier catches forty winks in a subway car.

on the emotional crowd, the tiny diva, dressed in her USO uniform and standing behind an NBC microphone, sang the "Marseillaise" to the twenty thousand who had come here to celebrate the liberation of Paris.

On October 1, the Stage Door Canteen welcomed its millionth serviceman. Ten days later, the day before Columbus Day, Times Square was the scene of a riot. Fortunately, there were no cops with clubs, just a bunch of hired security guards wondering how to handle thirty thousand teenagers who had formed a line around the Paramount Theater to hear a skinny crooner from Hoboken. The teenagers, many of whom were breaking the new curfew, were now called "bobbysoxers," a name derived from the ankle socks many of their mothers wore in the war plants. Lieutenant Commander Langfield was in the audience that day. He recalls, "Our ship was in the Brooklyn Navy Yard so I took the subway to Times Square. I knew Frank Sinatra as the kid who sang with Tommy Dorsey. I had no idea he had become so popular." As an officer, Langfield had no problem getting a ticket. "It was about eleven in the morning and I was sitting in the theater. All of a sudden all of these bobbysoxers began pouring in. I couldn't figure out what was going on. When he came on the stage pandemonium broke loose. They were dancing in the aisles and screaming."

There was one last wartime New Year's Eve in Times Square. For the 750,000 who showed up on December 31, 1944, that light at the end of the tunnel could not have been more palpable. At one minute before midnight, the glowing great white globe began to make its way down the pole in front of the Times Tower and when it reached its destination, the numbers "1945" glimmered in the night sky.

For the servicemen and servicewomen who passed through New York City during the war years, Times Square would leave them with some wonderful memories. Lunch at the Automat if they were solo, Toffenetti's if they had a date; there was a movie for every night of the week and a Broadway show that civilians would wait weeks to see. Meanwhile, taking a page from the yet-to-be-written musical *On the Town*, the Stage Door Canteen invited servicemen to cast the deciding vote in a contest to select "Miss New York" for the Atlantic City Beauty Pageant. Just one more gesture that helped make New York City one helluva town.

THE BOY DRESSED UP AS HITLER IS ABOUT
to be "hanged" by his friend in Times Square.
Effigies of the defeated dictator were hanged
in every borough.

It's Over!

"A sailor came over to my brother and asked, 'Can I kiss your girl?' Everybody was kissing everybody else."

Doris Lipetz on V-J Day

"My God! Everyone was pouring out of their houses. They were screaming: 'The War is over! They're coming home!' I can't begin to tell you the feeling it gave us."

Evelyn Lewis

It was the afternoon of April 12, 1945, and Miss Beatrice Lillie was standing in the wings of the Stage Door Canteen awaiting her cue. The British comedienne, who was about to perform a skit in the *Seven Lively Arts*, had her eyes on the director when he suddenly raised his hand, signaling the orchestra to stop. Everything went silent as he spoke: "I have a terrible announcement to make, but out of respect to the memory of

the President of the United States this show cannot go on." The soldiers and sailors in the audience stared uncomprehendingly at him until he realized he hadn't told them what happened. The words that were about to sear this date in their memory were spoken: "The President has just died."

Servicemen who weren't stunned into silence were sobbing as they shuffled out into the early evening. When they emerged into Times Square, they mingled with others who had heard the shocking news and were leaving movie houses and theaters. Fifteen-year-old Tom McLaughlin was walking down Broadway shortly after the news had reached New Yorkers. "People were coming toward me with tears streaming down their faces. I hadn't realized what his death meant until I saw those faces." It was rush hour, and people were surfacing from the subway station asking those who

had not been underground if it was true. Some got the news in the buses and trolley cars that were taking them home, and they, too, got off at Times Square hoping to be told that it was an unfounded rumor.

Then, when they looked up, they saw the flags on the Times Tower and the Hotel Astor flying at half-staff. Nearby firehouses sounded their alarms, and they knew that the president who had seen them through this war was dead.

Times Square became a somber place as nightclubs and hotel bars closed. Theatergoers didn't show up for their plays. Radio City Music Hall's matinee was abruptly halted as the stunned audience tried to take in the news. At Carnegie Hall, the philharmonic canceled its program and instead played the Funeral March from the Eroica Symphony and Richard Strauss's "A Hero's Life."

As it had been with Pearl Harbor, New Yorkers throughout the city would remember where they were when they heard the news:

Isabelle Sefton: "I was working out at La Guardia Air Field as a personnel interviewer for Pan American World Airways. We were in a car going home when the news came over the radio. Everybody was shocked. Utterly shocked."

Jack Gold: "We lived on the Upper West Side of Manhattan. Everybody was running outside, coming out of their homes. There were crowds on the streets. People were standing along the curbs as if they were waiting for a miracle. I'd never seen anything like it."

Evelyn Margulies: "I lived on Eastern Parkway. I heard the news on the radio at home. My parents had a fur store downstairs and I went to tell them. They already knew. Everybody was crying."

Louis Dienes: "I lived in Manhattan on Avenue A and 11th Street. I cried when I heard the news. I grew up listening to his Fireside Chats with my family. We loved him. He was a very strong president and when he died I felt very deeply. I was very affected by it."

Edna Satenstein: "I was standing on 229th Street and Carpenter Avenue. People had gathered in the street. Everyone was crying. People were saying, 'Oh, my God! Now we're going to have Truman.' Everybody was hysterical. We were getting this haberdasher. What in hell did he know?"

Miki Rosen: "We lived in the Bronx. At five o'clock, we'd stop playing outside and come in to listen to Tom Mix and his Ralston Straight Shooters on the radio. I went into the kitchen and told my mother. She didn't believe me."

Joseph Dash: "It was so devastating to me and to everyone we knew. We were walking around like zombies, not believing this could happen to our God. That's how we looked upon FDR."

Norman Corwin: "I was working at CBS. The word passed around: 'The President has died.' I went to a radio in time to hear, 'The funeral will be in the East Room.' It was an absolute shock. We were so accustomed to FDR. After all, he was elected four times. He had seen us through this war. It was as if your father had died."

Two days later, on April 14, at five minutes before 4:00 in the afternoon, the hour when the president's funeral service was to begin in the White House, the entire city stood still. Trolley cars stopped and subway cars were halted between stations. Planes scheduled to take off at La Guardia Field remained on the ground and in the Times Tower the presses that rolled out the news were silenced. Stores, theaters, and restaurants had been closed all day, but now as a light rain fell across the streets and sidewalks, there was a collective hush. People gathered in groups on Wall Street and along Fifth Avenue—wherever they happened to be—needing to share this new sorrow. In Times Square, as the minute hand on people's watches reached twelve, men and women, some of them elderly, dropped to their knees. Soldiers and sailors, a few resting on canes, stood absolutely still.

At 4:36 the following morning, the president's funeral train pulled into Pennsylvania Station, where its engine was changed for the final journey to Hyde Park. Had it been a New York Central train, the railroad might have attached the bar-lounge observation car of the new *Empire State Express*. In 1942 when it made its debut, the car was christened the *Franklin D. Roosevelt*, no doubt as a friendly salute to the president's penchant for mixing cocktails for his White House guests. Just two weeks later, on May 1, a few minutes before 5:00 on another rainy afternoon, New Yorkers walking past the Times Tower's bulletin board at 43rd Street saw a headline that brought neither tears nor cheers. Most people who read it quietly gloated. Some shrugged their shoulders and then moved on. The headline read:

HITLER IS DEAD

The man most hated by the free world didn't even rate an exclamation point. Even the extra editions bannering his death weren't grabbed from newsstand piles. The *New York Times* sent some of its reporters around the city to get reaction.

> *I would often walk from Hunter College on 68th Street to 53rd Street to catch the subway. On a night when Roosevelt was going to speak we didn't want to miss it, so we'd stop in a coffee shop, have a cup of coffee, and listen to it on the radio. We hung on every word. I couldn't wait to become old enough to vote for him.*
>
> —URSULA URSPRUNG

In Times Square, a cop on the beat looked up at the bulletin. "So, the bum's dead, eh? What difference does it make now?" A man who owned a monument yard on Ludlow Street said, "His headstone should be a skunk." Then he thought about it. "But he shouldn't be buried. He will contaminate the good earth." Several servicemen were waiting for a train in Pennsylvania Station when one of them spoke for the rest, "We'd like to spit on his grave, the _____." In the Brownsville section of Brooklyn, Joe Sisselman was washing dishes in Hoffman's Cafeteria when he heard the news. He commented, "Maybe it will save the lives of some of our American kids. For me it comes too late." Just ten days before, the dishwasher's son

was killed in Germany. Mayor La Guardia was returning to Manhattan from Brooklyn when he heard of the death of his nemesis. "That's the best news I've heard," he shouted into the two-way radio in his police car. "Look for anything to happen now."

The next day, in anticipation of the end of the war with Germany, the police began erecting barricades in front of glass-windowed storefronts in Times Square. Meanwhile, efforts continued to fund what was left of the war. In Rockefeller Center, a wooden replica of *The Fighting Lady*, an aircraft carrier being

NEW YORKERS gather around the *New York Times* news zipper. This scene was a familiar one during the war years as people waited anxiously to learn of the war's progress.

SOME OF THE 25,000 WHO HAD GATHERED in Times Square on May 7, 1945, to celebrate Germany's surrender.

built at the Brooklyn Navy Yard for action in the Pacific, was lowered into the sunken plaza. As part of the war bond drive, anyone who bought a bond could tour the carrier. The following week, a fifty-foot statue commemorating the Iwo Jima flag-raising was due to arrive in Times Square, to be placed in front of Lady Liberty.

Days before news of Hitler's death reached America, a rumor spread that Germany had surrendered. On the evening of April 28, as the news traveled across the city, more than ten thousand people gathered in Times Square. People gathered around the Times Tower's zipper awaiting more news, but a citywide "brownout" ordered on February 1 to preserve the country's dwindling coal supply had kept the moving electric sign dark. By 9:00, the first editions of Sunday's newspapers hit the streets and they all carried news of Germany's surrender. It wasn't until President Truman went on the air denying the surrender that crowds began to disperse.

Now, with Hitler dead and the war with Germany all but over, the city waited. Plans were put into place to have the official ceremonies held on Central Park's Mall. If word came by day, the ceremonies would run from 5:00 to 10:00 that night. If Germany's surrender wasn't announced until the evening, the ceremonies would be held the following day. It was President Truman's wish that the day not be spent in celebration, but in reflection and prayer. He reminded the nation that only one half of the war was over, with Japan still to be defeated. Meanwhile, Police Commissioner Lewis J. Valentine ordered over fifteen thousand of New York City's finest mobilized. Although a February 26 midnight curfew on bars and nightclubs to save on electricity had been lifted, the Hotel Association of New York City was asking its members to place a twenty-four-hour moratorium on the sale of liquor once Germany's surrender was announced.

At 9:35 on the morning of May 7, a Monday when most New Yorkers were just getting down to their jobs, a handful of people were standing around the Times Tower. They were watching the bulletins posted on the side of the building when the one the city had been waiting for was put up. At the same time, people listening to their radios heard the news. Word of mouth spread quickly, and by 11:30 an estimated crowd of 25,000 had jammed the Times Square subway station, trying to make their way to the sidewalk. The New York Telephone Company recorded the busiest day in its history as New Yorkers spread the news. Down on Wall Street, workers streamed out of their offices and gathered on the narrow sidewalks. At 10:30, the bells of Trinity Church pealed over the financial district. The church kept its doors open all day for continuing services. Churches and synagogues in every borough were filled with people offering thanks. Crowds gathered in Rockefeller Center, in the garment district, and in different pockets of the city. By noon, Times Square was closed off to traffic. As the day went on, half a million people would gather in the square, waiting.

It was a strange day. Amidst the collective relief, the city was still in mourning, its flags flying at half-staff for the president who had guided them through this war. Battles were still being fought in the Pacific, and President Truman had not yet told the American people that the war with Germany was over. That afternoon, the new president went on the air and declared that he would not officially proclaim V-E Day until he could do it simultaneously with England and Russia. That was good enough news for the people who now gathered in the nearest pub to toast a few. New Yorkers and the sailors and soldiers they were hosting needed to blow off some steam. For many in the lunch-hour crowd, that lunch would be liquid as they headed for the nearest taverns. By evening, bars and restaurants in Times Square ran out of beer. Some bars were so jammed, they had to close their doors to new customers until a few of the patrons who had

had enough decided to leave. Nightclubs had to call in waiters who had the day off to keep up with the growing crowd. Down on the Lower East Side, a small crowd was erecting an effigy of Hitler in the middle of Madison Street. "They needed a pair of pants for the dummy," remembers Martin Meyers, who was eleven years old. "My father was a waiter and I ran home and got his working pants. I nearly got killed for that." In the East New York section of Brooklyn, both ends of Milford Street were blocked off with big trash cans and a couple of rusty hot-water boilers. "Someone had gotten hold of a huge German flag and spread it out on the street," remembers Alan Walden, who skated across it.

The following morning New Yorkers gathered around radios in homes, in offices, and in war plants to hear President Truman announce the unconditional surrender of Germany. In the harbor, boats blasted their horns and in the city streets, cars honked and trolleys rang their bells.

I was fourteen. My friend and I took the subway to Times Square to see the celebration. We found our way to the roof of the Hotel Astor. From there we gazed out on a sea of humanity caught up in euphoric mass hysteria. The tremendous crowds were yelling and screaming, dancing and hugging. It was a once-in-a-lifetime experience.

—TOM MCLAUGHLIN

But the real celebration would come that night when the War Production Board officially ended the nationwide brownout. For the first time since April 1942, New York City could turn on its lights!

As the skies darkened, crowds poured into Times Square, hungry for its neon. Anticipating this moment, Douglas Leigh had, just a week ago, finished replacing the lights he had carefully stored away since his great signs went dark. The night before, the electric zipper on the Times Tower had resumed its swift crawl around the building. By dusk tonight, theater marquees, including the Paramount's and the Loews State's, and the neon signs on all the movie houses were lit up in their original state of dazzle. Then, at 8:00, the Lady in the Harbor had her torch lit. Although it was never fully extinguished—its handful of incandescent lights served as a guide to airplanes—it now shone with twice its pre-war glow.

But it was the lighting of Times Square's spectaculars that would give New

ALTHOUGH PRESIDENT TRUMAN WOULD not proclaim V-E Day until he could do so with England and Russia, crowds continued to grow in Times Square on May 7.

THE B-25 BOMBER WAS FLYING AT LESS THAN half the authorized altitude when it crashed into the Empire State Building on July 28, 1945. Had the accident occurred on a weekday when most offices were filled with workers, the casualties would have been higher.

Yorkers their city back. Suddenly at the square's north end, the Four Roses sign flashed on. Then came the Pepsi-Cola sign, its red, white, and blue colors warming people's hearts. The crowd couldn't contain themselves. "They're light happy!" shouted a sergeant who was being swept away by the tide of revelers. As confetti streamed down onto the square, a group of servicemen from other countries formed a ring in front of the Hotel Astor and sang "God Bless America."

The next morning, as sanitation trucks swept through the city, picking up the ribbons of ticker tape and scraps from torn telephone books that, in spite of the paper shortage, had streamed down on the streets the night before, an exhausted city began to focus on the sweetest day of all: the day when victory was declared against Japan.

In June, as the city was making plans to sell all ten of its giant air-raid sirens installed at strategic places during the war, U.S. Air Force B-29 bombers hit the city of Osaka in a series of raids, and by the middle of that month, Japan's second-largest industrial city was destroyed. Then, on June 21, the Battle of Okinawa—the largest, bloodiest land-air-sea battle in history—which had begun on the first day of April, dealt Japan a shattering defeat. It seemed to be a matter of time before the war would be over.

It was an overcast morning in July, the last Saturday of the month. Some New Yorkers were in Macy's catching up on their shopping. A few who had Saturday jobs were emerging from Pennsylvania Station or the nearby subway on their way to work. Eleanor Buscaglia was in the backyard of the house she lived in on 30th Street just off Ninth Avenue, hanging wash. At eleven minutes to ten she heard an ear-splitting explosion. Even though Hitler was already dead, her first thought was that somehow one of his planes had managed to cross the Atlantic and drop a bomb on a nearby building. Eleanor was not altogether wrong. Although the Luftwaffe had nothing to do with it, a twin-engine B-25 Army bomber had just crashed into the north wall of the Empire State Building, wedging its flaming carcass into the seventy-eighth and seventy-ninth floors.

Thousands of New Yorkers were eyewitnesses to the plane's desperate attempts to evade the city's skyscrapers as it tried to make its way in the blinding fog. The bomber had left Bedford, Massachusetts, and was en route to Newark Airport. It had just flown over La Guardia Field when the control tower radioed the pilot: "We're unable to see the top of the Empire State. Suggest you land here."

The pilot pushed on, entering Manhattan airspace at 50th Street when he found himself flying blind in a jungle of skyscrapers. The roar of the plane's engines bouncing off the office buildings startled people on the street. It also brought office workers to their windows. Those on high floors looked out to see the wayward plane actually flying below them! As the bomber headed southwest, Army Air Force Lieutenant Frank Covey, who was staying at the Biltmore Hotel, looked out of his window just as the plane was heading toward the twenty-second floor of the Grand Central Office Building, which straddles Park Avenue at 46th Street. The plane quickly banked, evading the building as it headed west, narrowly missing another building at Fifth Avenue and 42nd Street before turning south. It was now seconds away from its fateful end. Stan Lomax, a sportscaster for radio station WOR, was driving to work when he heard the roar of the plane's motors directly overhead. Looking up from his car window, he shouted, "Climb, you fool, climb!" just as the plane thundered into the Empire State Building.

The impact was spectacular. Ten tons of steel traveling at a speed of two hundred miles an hour and carrying a full load of high-octane fuel slammed into the limestone facade. The massive 102-story tower shuddered under the incredible force, which jettisoned one of the plane's engines down an elevator shaft, where it landed in the basement. The other engine went through seven solid walls before emerging from the 33rd Street side of the building, landing in the penthouse studio of sculptor Henry Hering. Giant fireballs melted walls and metal furniture and incinerated those in their path. Fourteen people, including the plane's three occupants, perished in the flames. Because it was a Saturday, most offices were closed. One of the exceptions was the War Relief Services of the National Catholic Welfare

I came home on the Queen Mary *in August. We came through the Narrows just as news of the bombing of Nagasaki reached us. There was a ticker-tape parade for us when we reached Pier 90. It was thrilling to arrive here just as the war was coming to an end. I had never seen the Statue of Liberty. To come up that river and see the statue, to dock and have everybody running to greet you, that was thrilling.*

—JACK WAYMAN,
30TH INFANTRY DIVISION

THE SIGHT OF THE *QUEEN MARY* sailing up the Narrows into New York Harbor on June 20, 1945, thrilled New Yorkers who came out to welcome her. On the ocean liner were nearly fifteen thousand returning servicemen and women.

Conference, whose offices on the north side of the building's seventy-ninth floor were directly in the plane's deadly path. From fifteen to twenty members of its staff were working that Saturday, and of those, only five survived.

It was early August, and like the rest of the country, New York City was counting the weeks until the Japanese would surrender. If news of their defeats in the Pacific wasn't enough to convince the most cautious-minded New Yorker, rumors were circulating that the Soviet Union was about to declare war on Japan. Then, at 10:45 on the morning of August 6, President Truman issued a statement telling the American people that sixteen hours earlier, "about the time that

SHIPS OF THE RETURNING
United States fleet can be seen from 96th Street and
Riverside Drive on October 26, 1945, as they make their way up the Hudson.

citizens on the Eastern seaboard were sitting down to their Sunday suppers," an American plane had dropped an atomic bomb on the Japanese city of Hiroshima.

The president described the city as "an important army base." The War Department was unable to describe the damage inflicted because of "an impenetrable cloud of dust and smoke" that settled over the bomb's target, although anyone reading about the steel tower that had been "vaporized" during a test run three weeks earlier in the New Mexico desert would understand what had just occurred.

The 8,900-pound uranium bomb that destroyed Hiroshima was incubated in a bed of fear. In 1939, President Roosevelt received a letter from three German-Jewish scientists who had fled to the United States when Hitler became chancellor. Among them was Albert Einstein. In the letter, they warned the president that scientists in Nazi Germany were at work on the use of uranium to produce an atomic bomb. Out of that fear emerged the Manhattan Project, which had its beginnings on a cold evening in January 1939 when three scientists, working five stories below street level in Columbia University's Pupin Physics Laboratories at Broadway and 120th Street, split the free world's first atom. Carlyn Parker, who was married to a naval officer stationed at Columbia, worked in that laboratory as part of a team separating uranium: "One day everybody was ordered to go down to the basement. There in a large trough between two heavy concrete slabs was a long slender object. It was the beginning of what would become the first atom bomb."

By 1942, the Manhattan Project was recruiting top scientists throughout the free world. Uranium was needed and the man to see was Edgar Sengier, managing director of one of the biggest uranium mines in the Belgium Congo. From his office in the Cunard Building at 25 Broadway, Sengier informed General Leslie Groves, who headed the project, that the uranium he needed was not in deepest Africa, but sitting in a warehouse in the Port Richmond section of Staten Island! Worried about the ore's safety once Europe was at war, Sengier had moved 1,250 tons of uranium

> *I spent seven, eight months on a troop transport, bringing ships back from Southampton to New York. We had five and six thousand troops coming home every time. We seized the* Europa *from the Nazis. They used it as a stable, so we had to clean it up and get it ready for the troops who were coming back home. When the troops came off the ship they were yelling and screaming and crying. All the families were there to meet them.*
>
> — SAM LEVINE

NEW YORKERS REGULARLY LINED THE CITY piers as ships with returning troops got ready to offload their precious cargo.

to New York City. A second warehouse, at 20th Street off the West Side Highway, also held the precious metal.

The Manhattan Project was appropriately named: it turned out that the city's piers, warehouses, and offices would be very important to the super-secret project where things had to be hidden "in plain sight." The Woolworth Building in the shadow of City Hall provided a "front company" on the eleventh, twelfth, and fourteenth floors. Scientists passing as businessmen worked here on uranium's rare isotope, a vital component of making the bomb. But it was an unassuming building on the southwest corner of Chambers Street overlooking City Hall Park that would become Ground Zero. From here, on the building's eighteenth floor, the Army Corps of Engineers would not only direct atom research, it would eventually build whole "hidden nuclear cities" in Tennessee, New Mexico, and Washington State. Many of those who were hired to work in these invented cities situated in the middle of nowhere had no idea that they were helping to build a nuclear bomb.

By the time three of the bombs were tested three years later at Alamogordo, New Mexico, Hitler was dead and Germany had surrendered. Seventy scientists, among them Leo Szilard and James Franck, who had both worked on the project, signed a petition opposing the use of the bomb on moral grounds. But after the initial Japanese turndown of the Potsdam Declaration issued on July 26 laying the ground rules for surrender, Harry Truman decided to proceed. New Yorkers had conflicting feelings about the decision. "I was horrified," said Louis Dienes. "By the time V-E Day came we knew that Japan was defeated. The news of the dropping of the atomic bomb was electrifying. Thirty thousand people were killed instantaneously." Martha Yamasaki, who later met some of the victims, was angry: "I thought America did a very bad thing. You can't boast that you're peaceful if you bomb innocent women and children." Fourteen-year-old Edna Satenstein discussed it in school the following day: "That was a pretty frightening thing. It was accepted and not accepted. Yet people said it ended the war."

It was early morning on August 11 when the great ship sailed into the Narrows. Not only did all of New York know she was arriving, the *Queen Elizabeth* was at the front of a parade of five other troop transports bringing the soldiers home. What a difference from her maiden voyage five years earlier, when she arrived here on that fog-shrouded morning, in secret, without escort! On this Saturday, New Yorkers lined the shores of Brooklyn and Staten Island, waving and shouting a rousing welcome. Fireboats hovering near the Statue of Liberty sprayed their delicate geysers into the air as ferryboats and tugboats blasted their whistles. On her deck soldiers, and army nurses, sailors, and marines cheered as the New York skyline loomed before them. Just two months before, on June 20, the *Queen Mary* arrived—the first of the returning troopships—delivering nearly fifteen thousand servicemen and servicewomen from a defeated Germany. The soldiers and sailors on the *Queen Elizabeth* began their transatlantic journey believing this was to be a furlough. Then news of the atomic bombs on Hiroshima and Nagasaki reached them, followed by Russia's declaration of war on Japan. Finally, they were informed that the Japanese were close to accepting the terms of the Potsdam Declaration, and they knew they were on a one-way ticket home.

The city where they arrived was tense with expectation. Servicemen congregated in the servicemen's lounges in Pennsylvania Station and Grand Central

A CROWD GATHERS AROUND
the Times Building in Times Square, waiting for word of
Japan's surrender to come across the news zipper.

Terminal, staying close to the radio as they waited for Truman to make an announcement. The one group already celebrating were Japanese-Americans, some of whom had already been relocated to hostels in the city after being released from West Coast relocation centers. Not only would their families in Japan be safe from further bombing, they would be able to find jobs again in their adopted country. Meanwhile, returning troopships continued to arrive in New York Harbor, some of them on Staten

LOOKING DOWN TIMES SQUARE AT THE CROWD THAT
had gathered on the night of August 15, 1945, to
celebrate the end of war with Japan.

clockwise from top: Lots of sailors kissed lots of young women on V-J Day; Crowds spill out of this East Harlem tenement on 107th Street to celebrate the end of the war; A Chinese newspaper vendor in Chinatown holds a copy of the *China Tribune* announcing the Japanese surrender.

Island, as cheering crowds lined the piers and the parks along the waterfront to welcome them. Mel Edelstein, a six-year-old Brooklynite, saw some of those ships. He recalls, "We'd take the subway to Manhattan and the train would go over the Manhattan Bridge. I remember looking down at New York Bay and there were hundreds, maybe thousands of ships bringing men back from Europe." How long had it been since New Yorkers could look up at their skies and see squadrons of planes delivering not harm, but returning American troops? Because WNEW's

WHEN NEWS OF JAPAN'S IMMINENT SURRENDER ARRIVED,
a group of New Yorkers gathered at Madison Square in lower Manhattan for an
impromptu parade.

50,000-watt radio signal was so strong, pilots used the station's frequency to guide them as they flew toward New York City. How sweet it must have been for returning troops to be able to listen to the popular radio station as they arrived home!

On Monday, August 13, President Truman went to bed early, but

A RETURNING soldier kisses his wife outside their third-floor apartment at 3027 42nd Street, Astoria, Queens. The building is still standing.

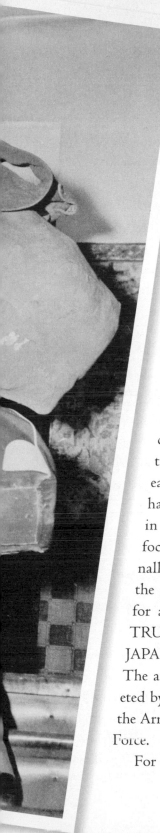

not before announcing to the country that even though Japan had accepted the unconditional surrender demand of the Allies, no confirmation would be forthcoming before 9:00 the following morning. By dawn, a large crowd had gathered in front of the Times Tower's electric news zipper, keeping an informal vigil as the city waited. The crowd grew as morning turned to afternoon. By early evening an estimated half million people were in the square, their eyes focused on the zipper. Finally, at 7:03 P.M., the words the nation had been waiting for appeared: OFFICIAL— TRUMAN ANNOUNCES JAPANESE SURRENDER. The announcement was bracketed by three stars representing the Army, the Navy, and the Air Force.

For twenty minutes a continuous roar rang out in the square. Hats flew into the air and strangers embraced. Doris Lipetz was there, and remembers, "It was absolutely jammed. There were no cars going through. People were dancing and singing in the street." By 10:00, two million people had gathered in Times Square. Nightclubs couldn't handle the crowds that surged inside. The Copa had twice as many patrons as usual squeezing around its tiny tables. At the Zanzibar, diners stood on tables, screaming for joy when the news was heard. Four doormen were posted in front of the Stork Club to prevent revelers from crashing the nightclub's exclusive celebration.

Every section of the city and every borough had their way of welcoming the news. In Chinatown, four large symbolic dragons usually brought out for the Chinese New Year led processions through the narrow streets. Every fire escape on the old tenement buildings was filled with Chinese families waving flags and cheering, while below them the sacred dragon dance symbolizing peace wended its way around the neighborhood. "Brooklyn exploded into block parties," says Joan Harris. "We all carried tables into the street, brought food down and celebrated into the night." Nineteen-year-old Bea Levine, who lived in East New York, remembers neighbors gathering on their stoops, banging pots and pans: "We would hit those pots with our wooden spoons. It was wonderful!" There were more block parties in the Bronx. "It was a wonderful day," remembers Edna Satenstein. "It was a wonderful day and it was a sad day because so many soldiers from our neighborhood were killed." Emotions ran high all over the city. "In my neighborhood you could have floated boats on the amount of tears being shed that day," remembers Bronx-born Joseph Dash, who grew up on the Grand Concourse. Mary Shalo was living on Staten Island. She says, "The church bells were ringing. Lights were blazing and people were cheering in the streets." Every church and synagogue in all five boroughs was filled with people giving thanks. From his new home in Gracie Mansion, Mayor La Guardia went on the city's radio station WNYC and announced that he was designating Wednesday and Thursday as "Victory Days." Every office and department store, and all city departments except those necessary to keep the city functioning, were closed for business.

It wasn't until September 2, as the Japanese representatives signed the Instrument of Surrender on the USS *Missouri*, that President Truman declared the war with Japan to be officially over. Just a few cheers went up when the news bulletin came across the Times Tower's electric zipper at 10:04 that night. For New Yorkers, the days and nights of wild celebration were behind them. It was the beginning of the Labor Day weekend, the first in four years when New Yorkers were no longer living under the shadow of war. Gas was back in the pumps, the weatherman promised some sunshine, and what more American way was there to celebrate this final end to the Second World War than to pack up the car and head for the beach?

We Couldn't Have Done It Without Them

★ ★

Every one of the city's five boroughs played a valiant role in the war effort, and while Manhattan is and was then the Center of the Universe, two other boroughs helped shape America's role in the war and were instrumental in its victory. Because they were "kissing cousins" separated by Lower New York Bay—the slender channel that protects New York Harbor—Brooklyn and Staten Island have always been vital components to the geography of New York City. It was

THE BROOKLYN WATERFRONT was vital to the war effort. At the massive grain terminal in the Gowanus section, grain is discharged directly into ships.

from the Brooklyn side of the Narrows at Fort Hamilton where on July 4, 1776, an American soldier fired a battery of cannon shots at British man-of-war ships approaching the city. The British got their revenge a short time later when they landed at Fort Wadsworth on the Staten Island side of the Narrows, launching the battle that would lead to their seven-year occupation of New York City.

Fast forward to World War II, when the Brits and the Americans were on the same side. Between Fort Wadsworth and Fort Hamilton, an underwater net was strung to keep U-boats from entering the harbor. It was kept open until the Navy's hydrophones—subterranean listening equipment connected to stations on shore—detected something suspicious. Up above, both waterfronts were humming with activity. Rising along the Brooklyn waterfront in Upper New York Bay was one of the most important complexes involved in the war effort. The New York Port of Embarkation, now known as the Brooklyn Army Terminal, was a virtual naval city of piers, docks, and warehouses from which half of the East Coast's Europe-bound cargo was dispatched. The army terminal was also one of the largest processing centers for servicemen. Every soldier who trained in an eastern camp was shipped off to war from here. Fort Hamilton also processed soldiers and at the war's peak, between them, 100,000 troops left Brooklyn every day of the week for battlefields in Europe and Africa. Farther north, opposite Governor's Island, is Red Hook, where the Todd Shipyards built the landing crafts that carried American troops onto the beaches of Normandy. And there was the Brooklyn Navy Yard, the 290-acre site surrounding Wallabout Bay in the Williamsburg section, where battleships were built, repaired, and supplied. To protect this precious collection, anti-aircraft installations were placed atop several of Brooklyn's buildings, un-

seen by the average Brooklynite. What the citizens of that borough did see and had to get used to were the gun emplacements installed in many of their parks. Anti-aircraft batteries were sometimes moved from one area to another, depending on where they were needed.

Like Brooklyn, Staten Island's waterfront during World War II was a beehive of shipyards, docks, and warehouses, all geared to the war effort. At its northern edge along Mariner's Cove, the Bethlehem Steel plant employed twelve thousand workers around the clock to build destroyers. Every propeller for the ships built in all of its other yards was made here as well. Along Upper New York Bay, Stapleton was home to an army embarkation center, and nearby Tompkinsville was the place where a young Staten Islander unknowingly welcomed a famous visitor to New York.

It was early dawn on May 11, 1943. The day before, fifteen-year-old Mickey Carbonella had been working the docks in Stapleton when his boss told him to show up at 4:00 the next morning at a particular dock in nearby Tompkinsville. When Mickey arrived he could see a large ship moored in the middle of the Narrows. "We're going out on that ship," his boss told him. When Mickey asked who was out there he got no answer. The two slipped into a dinghy and headed out to the vessel. As they approached her, Mickey could see a group of seamen on the top deck beginning to make their way down the stairs. With them was a man dressed in civilian clothes with a blanket pulled over his head. The man remained shrouded and silent as he and his seamen boarded the dinghy. In the predawn darkness, Mickey noticed a lighted ember poking from the blanket. He then realized that the man was smoking a cigar. The dinghy approached the dock at Tompkinsville and the man was helped out, at which point he removed the blanket from his head. Mickey found himself staring into the face of Winston Churchill. In 1943, at the height of the war, the British prime minister's journey across the U-boat–infested Atlantic had to be kept secret. From New York, Churchill would board a train to Washington, D.C., for a meeting with President Roosevelt. It pleased Mickey Carbonella, who would later enlist in the army, to know that the prime minister's first stop on American soil was Staten Island.

CROWDS GATHER IN TIMES SQUARE to ring in 1946, the first year when the country was no longer at war. Lights are back on Broadway and the new year would soon be ushered in with the familiar dropping ball, now glowing with light.

Epilogue

It was an exhilarating time and an uncertain time. Great joy and deep sorrow were each fueled by hope and not a little faith. The war had torn a hole in the city's life and now, with victory, a word that was still fresh on our lips, the past and the future had some catching up to do. Three days before New Yorkers erupted in a spasm of joy to celebrate the war's end, a small article appeared in the *New York Times* that foretold one of the ways the face of the city would change. Joseph Platzker, New York City's housing commissioner, had been trying to find a home for Mayor La Guardia now that he was about to leave Gracie Mansion and become a private citizen. After searching the city from Greenwich Village to the Riverdale section of the Bronx, the commissioner threw up his hands and muttered, "No success." If the mayor couldn't find a home, what would become of the thousands of servicemen disembarking from those troopships—many of them married and anxious to start families—who needed a place to live?

La Guardia had already put his powerful parks commissioner,

put at the top of the renting list. Stuyvesant Town was a radical idea for its time, with lots of pros and cons. True, the project leveled some pretty dilapidated tene-

Robert Moses, on the case, and in 1943 Moses had formed a partnership between the city and the Metropolitan Life Insurance Company. Together they would build a cluster of red brick buildings—enough to house 8,757 families—in what had been a depressed area on the Lower East Side that once held the city's massive and odorous gas tanks. Eighteen city blocks and stores were leveled for this middle-class enclave stretching east from First Avenue between 14th and 20th streets, where servicemen were

ments, but those tenements had formed a neighborhood of 3,100 families, their churches, schools, and shops. The apartments were airy, spacious, and pleasant. And even if their architecture evoked state prisons, they were situated on lovely lawns with shade trees where children could safely play—that is, if the children were white. Black servicemen and their families were not permitted in Stuyvesant Town. They were directed to the Riverton Houses, another middle-income housing development being built by Met

Life, this one on a twelve-acre lot running north from 135th to 138th Street and stretching from Fifth Avenue to the Harlem River.

"The projects" had been popping up in poor neighborhoods since the late 1930s, when the city created the New York City Housing Authority. Now, with returning veterans looking for places to live, many more of them were going up. Brooklyn got the Brownsville Houses in Brownsville and the Williamsburg Houses in Williamsburg. In East Harlem a ten-building complex went up and was named the James Weldon Johnson houses, after the African-American poet.

The 25th Street block in Chelsea between Ninth and Tenth avenues, which was used as a barracks for the U.S. Coast Guard during the war, became the site for the John Lovejoy Elliott Houses. On the Lower East Side, the Jacob Riis Houses replaced blocks of crumbling tenements. Turning their backs to the city's familiar grid, these projects redefined the cityscape, often to the displeasure of preservationists who felt that as the city tore down the old, pieces of its soul were being shoveled away in the rubble. Preservationists would have a difficult time in the next several decades as Robert Moses, using his famous My-way-IS-the-highway

THE BROWNSVILLE Housing Project was one of several low-income projects in Brooklyn where returning veterans could settle down.

approach, envisioned a city that was, to some, a giant exit ramp to the suburbs.

For many returning GIs, those suburbs represented sweet serenity, a place far removed from their all-too-fresh memories. But an affordable home seemed like a pipe dream, and even if they could scrape together the down payment, there were no houses to be had. One of those returning servicemen was a member of a family who happened to own four thousand acres of former potato fields in the town of Hempstead on Long Island. Lieutenant William Levitt convinced his father to subdivide the land and build mass-produced houses that could be rented cheaply to returning GIs. On May 7, 1947, Levitt and Sons went public with their plan to erect two thousand rental homes for veterans. Two days after an ad appeared in the papers, half of those homes were spoken for. Levittown was the country's first "instant suburb," and for young couples otherwise forced to live with their parents or rent out someone's attic, it was heaven. Photographer Arthur Leipzig moved his family into one. He says, "Our rent was $67 a month. We had two kids and my daughter was so thrilled by the freedom, she kept going in and out of doors." Like Stuyvesant Town, however, the rental of these houses was restricted to whites. Mimi Leipzig remembers her reaction: "If I was a black

I would have been in such a rage. They were good enough to fight and they couldn't find housing."

Returning Japanese-Americans had a particularly tough time in the city. "Kelly" Kuwayama saw signs that read "No Japs Allowed" and No Japs Wanted" outside employment offices. Some were denied service in stores and restaurants. This experience had to be particularly embittering in light of the bravery with which they performed their war duties, many of them coming home with bronze and silver stars. Martha Yamasaki was philosophical: "As Japanese-Americans, we were very lucky to be in New York City. My sister-in-law lived on the West Coast and her entire family was uprooted. They lost their fruit and vegetable business and were incarcerated for the duration of the war."

Even white men like Arthur Leipzig with nice houses in the suburbs had a tough time making ends meet: "I remember we had to scrape together money from recycling bottles so we could go into the city." As the machinery of war ground to a halt, unemployment offices in all five boroughs were jammed. One out-of-work waiter showed up at an unemployment office and said he wanted a job in a war plant. The guy behind the desk looked up. "A war plant? Haven't you heard? The war is over." The closings of the war plants with their high-paying jobs were hard on many of the women who had taken the place of the men who went to war. The ones who had taken jobs traditionally filled by men were told that, as soon as the war ended, they would have to relinquish them to the returning servicemen who had families to support. Many women took those jobs to help support their own families when their husbands were drafted. Now, some of those women found themselves widowed or with husbands who were facing a dismal job market.

President Roosevelt foresaw all of this and in 1944 he signed the GI Bill of Rights into law, guaranteeing, among other things, a free education for returning servicemen. September of 1945 was a busy time for New York City's colleges and the lines to register were long. Columbia University had already introduced a "peacetime training program" tailored to post-war students who were less interested in the campus experience than in getting an education that would help them get on with their interrupted lives. Even high school enrollment was at record levels, as the teenagers who had dropped out of high school to take war jobs in the city were now ready to resume their education. That September, Manhattan's Washington Irving High School, Flushing High School in Queens, and Midwood High School in Brooklyn all had registration lines that continued from morning into the late afternoon.

No doubt about it: the city was preparing itself for the future, and that future, when it arrived, would be exciting. In 1947, ground would be broken along a depressed section of the East River waterfront for the United Nations Headquarters, and the neighborhood that was once home to slaughterhouses would belong to the world. New York City would find itself referred to as the Paris of the Art World when American artist Jackson Pollock "dripped" his paints on canvases, catapulting abstract expressionism onto center stage. One of the artists in the movement was Max Ernst, the German-Jewish refugee whom Varian Fry rescued in 1940. Architecture would help tell the story of the city's date with the future as tall glass boxes loomed over the ornate, brick "wedding cake" office buildings whose stone gargoyles looked back at yesterday. The city was about to shed its skin, after all, leaving that war far behind.

But for a little while, New Yorkers needed to catch their breath and savor their city in this new peacetime. Just a week after V-J Day, on a hot day in August, five thousand youngsters lined up on Twelfth Avenue and 49th Street in front of Pier 88, where a captured U-boat was berthed. They had each brought ten pounds of paper in exchange for a ticket to board the German submarine. The children waited for hours to get on board. How thrilling it must have been to walk through the subdued monster that once sent freighters to the bottom of the sea! On September 8, in Atlantic City, Miss America was crowned. She was chosen by returning soldiers who had been prisoners of war in Germany. She was a Bronx girl, a graduate of Hunter College. Her name was Bess Myerson, and she was a Jew.

On November 1, Times Square's Stage Door Canteen closed its doors, and on the last Thursday of that month, the day that FDR had set aside for the holiday, Macy's Thanksgiving Day Parade was back with its famous balloons soaring above the skyscrapers. There was a turkey for every table, and Schrafft's was once again selling its famous pumpkin and mincemeat pies. Pennsylvania Station and Grand Central Terminal were jammed with soldiers and sailors, this time returning to their own homes for the holiday. A tradition was started on Park Avenue at Christmastime when twenty-nine fir trees were planted along the avenue's dividing island and lit to honor the war dead. The season was helping to bring color back to the city. Crowds filled Fifth Avenue, spilling into Saks, Lord & Taylor, and Best & Co., where their eyes could feast on things they hadn't seen during the war years. One could still ride up and down the avenue in

a double-decker bus. Those icons, built by the Fifth Avenue Coach Company, had another year to run before they would be retired, along with the city's trolleys. As if taking a cue from Irving Berlin's song, 1945 brought New York City a white Christmas. Snow covered the branches of the Rockefeller Center Christmas tree, softening the glow from the seven hundred globes that now blazed with light. The Christmas show at Radio City Music Hall was featuring Bing Crosby and Ingrid Bergman in *The Bells of St. Mary's*, and at Town Hall, the von Trapp Family, who had fled the Nazis in Austria to come to America, were singing Christmas carols.

Times Square has always been the city's outdoor cathedral for celebration, and this new year, the first that New Yorkers could ring in without war since 1941, the crowds gathered. Sobriety was not even a consideration as soldiers and sailors, remembering what battlefront they were on the New Year's Eve before, let whiskey carry them into tomorrow. The lighted ball made its slow run down the pole, the tin horns were tooting, the crowd was shouting, and the square's great spectaculars glowed into dawn.

The year 1946 would begin to distance the city not just from the war years, but from the time just before it, when silly-looking men capable of great evil strutted around Yorkville. There were no

A TRADITION WAS STARTED ON PARK
Avenue after the war when trees planted
along the center islands to honor the war
dead were decorated with Christmas lights.

more Jews in Germany to rhapsodize over the New York skyline, but the ones who had escaped and came to live here often found that this difficult, exasperating spot on the globe got under their skin. Austrian-born writer Ernst Waldinger devoted poems to the New York Elevated and the Battery. No sooner had playwright Ferdinand Bruckner left the city to work in Hollywood than he began counting the days until he could trade that "candy-coated hell" for the city's gritty streets. Writer Ferenc Molnár became so attached to his neighborhood—58th Street between Fifth and Sixth avenues—that he could never entertain the idea of moving, even one city block. And when Lore Segal, who wrote *Other People's Houses*, walked down 57th Street, a memory of a particular New York City experience triggered something: "It is, I think, the way our histories become charged thus upon the air, the streets, the very houses of New York, that makes the alien into a citizen." New York can do that to people.

Acknowledgments

★ ★

This book belongs, in large part, to the men and women whose stories brought life and meaning to it. I thank them for their memories: Norma Bock, Eleanor Buscaglia, Sylvia Buscaglia, Norman Corwin, Walter Cronkite, Phillip Curtin, Joseph Dash, David Diamant, Louis Dienes, Rocky Doino, Mel Edelstein, Robert F. Gallagher, Jack Gold, Yetta Guy, Joan Harris, Mollie Heckerling, Lily Hollander, Don Israel, Kathy Jolowicz, Larry Karlin, Werner Kleeman, Dorothy Koppelman, Raymond Langfield, Angela Lansbury, David Lawrence, Arthur Leipzig, Mimi Leipzig, Elinore Leo, Bea Levine, Sam Levine, Evelyn Lewis, Doris Lipetz, Carolina Madeo, Evelyn Margulies, Richard McDermott, Tom McLaughlin, Martin Meyers, Carlyn Parker, Charles Rodin, Miki Rosen, Edna Satenstein, Isabelle Sefton, Bill Shaw, Manny Soshensky, Fritz Stern, Henry Stern, Ethel Ursprung, Murray A. Valenstein, Bill Vericker, Frances Kelly Vericker, Alan Walden, Barbara Walters, Arthur H. Westing. Special thanks to Gary Lewi of the American Airpower Museum at Republic, New York, who put me in touch with those Riveting Rosies: Georgette Feller, Anne King, Connie Mancuso, Josephine Rachiele, and Sophie Sarro. Leslie Shreve led me to Susan Dorler, who introduced me to the Dutch Treaters: Sylvan Barnet, Ray Kintsler, Ray Stone, and Jack Wayman. Aileen Yamaguchi and Stanley Kanzaki at the New York Japanese American Citizens League put me in touch with Yeichi "Kelly" Kuwayama, Martha Yamasaki, and Fujio Saito. Mary Shalo and Larry Culley helped to shine a light on Staten Island's war effort.

Finding the best photographs to illustrate the text was made easier by Bill Bregoli; Melanie Bower and Faye Haun at the Museum of the City of New York; Eva Tucholka and the gang at Culver Pictures; Caroline Waddell at the United States Holocaust Memorial Museum; the Bob Hope Legacy; Matthew Lutts of the Associated Press; Angela Troisi of the *New York Daily News*; Ron Mandelbaum at Photofest; Kenneth Johnson and Lewis Wyman at the Library of Congress; Douglas DiCarlo at the La Guardia and Wagner Archives; Arthur Leipzig; Miranda Schwartz and Jill Slaight at the New-York Historical Society; Charles Sachs and Carey Stumm at the New York Transit Museum; Julie May at the Brooklyn Historical Society; MacKenzie Bennett at MOMA; Michael Massmann at Redux Pictures; and Christine Roussel at the Rockefeller Center Archives.

What started out as a gleam in my eye and a stirring of my imagination was given shape by my editor, Elisabeth Dyssegaard. Her enthusiasm was infectious and her guidance invaluable. I consider myself fortunate to have worked with her. Kathryn Antony's keen eye and good taste helped me choose the perfect images to illustrate this story. Of course, none of this would have happened had my agent, Ellen Levine, not seen the possibilities and worked her magic. And last but far from least, I give special thanks to my husband, Bill, who tackled the laborious job of helping to find and secure many of the photographs in this book. My job was made so much easier when he offered to help. That he did so with great patience and perseverance made me appreciate, even more, his generous gift to me.

Bibliography

★ ★

Ardman, Harvey. *Normandie: Her Life and Times.* New York: F. Watts, 1985.

Armstrong, Nancy. *The Rockefeller Center Christmas Tree: The History & Lore of the World's Most Famous Evergreen.* Kennebunkport, Maine: Cider Mill Press, 2008.

Arnot, Charles P. *"Don't Kill the Messenger": The Tragic Story of Welles Hangen and Other Journalistic Combat Victims.* New York: Vantage Press, 1994.

Bacall, Lauren. *By Myself.* New York: Alfred A. Knopf, 1978.

Belle, John, and Maxine R. Leighton. *Grand Central: Gateway to a Million Lives.* New York: W. W. Norton & Company, 2000.

Berczeller, Richard. *Displaced Doctor.* New York: The Odyssey Press, 1964.

Bloomfield, Gary. *Duty, Honor, Victory: America's Athletes in World War II.* Guilford, Connecticut: The Lyons Press, 2003.

Blum, John Morton. *V Was for Victory: Politics and American Culture during World War II.* New York: Harcourt Brace & Company, 1976.

Campbell, Rodney. *The Luciano Project: The Secret Wartime Collaboration of the Mafia & the U.S. Navy.* New York: McGraw-Hill Book Company, 1977.

Carlson, John Roy. *Under Cover: My Four Years in the Nazi Underworld of America—The Amazing Revelation of How Axis Agents and Our Enemies Within Are Now Plotting to Destroy the United States.* New York: E. P. Dutton & Co., 1943.

Chabon, Michael. *The Amazing Adventures of Kavalier & Clay.* New York: Picador, 2000.

Conant, Jennet. *The Irregulars: Roald Dahl and the British Spy Ring in Wartime Washington.* New York: Simon & Schuster, 2008.

Cooke, Alistair. *The American Home Front, 1941–1942.* New York: Grove Press, 2006.

Davis, Kenneth S. *FDR, Into the Storm: 1937–1940: A History.* New York: Random House, 1993.

Diamond, Sander A. *The Nazi Movement in the United States: 1924–1941.* Ithaca, New York: Cornell University Press, 1974.

Dobbs, Michael. *Saboteurs: The Nazi Raid on America.* New York: Alfred A. Knopf, 2004.

Duffy, James P. *Target America: Hitler's Plan to Attack the United States.* Guilford, Connecticut: First Lyons Press, 2004.

Francisco, Charles. *The Radio City Music Hall: An Affectionate History of the World's Greatest Theater.* New York: E. P. Dutton, 1979.

Frank, Wolfgang. *The Sea Wolves: The Story of German U-Boats at War.* New York: Rinehart & Company, 1955.

Fromm, Bella. *Blood and Banquets: A Berlin Social Diary.* London: Geoffrey Bles, 1943.

Gabler, Neal. *Winchell: Gossip, Power and the Culture of Celebrity.* New York: Alfred A. Knopf, 1994.

Gannon, Michael. *Operation Drumbeat: The Dramatic True Story of Germany's First U-Boat Attacks Along the American Coast in World War II.* New York: Harper & Row Publishers, 1990.

Gelernter, David. *1939: The Lost World of the Fair.* New York: The Free Press, 1995.

Gilbert, Bill. *They Also Served: Baseball and the Home Front, 1941–1945.* New York: Crown Publishers, 1992.

Gilbert, Martin. *Churchill and America.* New York: The Free Press, 2005.

Girdner, Audrie and Anne Loftis. *The Great Betrayal: The Evacuation of the Japanese-Americans During World War II.* London: The Macmillan Company, 1969.

Goldstein, Richard. *Spartan Seasons: How Baseball Survived the Second World War.* New York: Macmillan Publishing Co., 1980.

Goodwin, Doris Kearns. *No Ordinary Time: Franklin and Eleanor Roosevelt: The Home Front in World War II.* New York: Simon & Schuster, 1994.

Gregory, Ross. *America 1941: America at the Crossroads.* New York: The Free Press, 1989.

Grover, Warren. *Nazis in Newark.* Edison, New Jersey: Transaction Publishers, 2003.

Gumpert, Martin. *First Papers.* New York: Duell, Sloan and Pearce, 1941.

Hanc, John. *Jones Beach: An Illustrated History.* Guilford, Connecticut: Globe Pequot Press, 2007.

Harris, Mark Jonathan; Franklin Mitchell, and Steven Schechter. *The Homefront.* New York: G.P. Putnam's Sons, 1984.

Heilbut, Anthony. *Exiled in Paradise: German Refugee Artists and Intellectuals in America from the 1930s to the Present.* Berkeley, California: University of California Press, 1983.

Hope, Bob. *Bob Hope Remembers . . . World War II:*

The European Theatre & D-Day, compiled and edited by Ward Grant. Burbank, California: Hope Enterprises, 1994.

Hoyt, Edwin P. *U-Boats Offshore: When Hitler Struck America*. New York: Stein and Day, 1978.

Jason, Philip K., and Iris Posner, editors. *Don't Wave Goodbye: The Children's Flight from Nazi Persecution to American Freedom*. Westport, Connecticut and London: Praeger, 2004.

Jeffers, H. Paul. *The Napoleon of New York: Mayor Fiorello LaGuardia*. New York: John Wiley & Sons, 2002.

Kessner, Thomas. *Fiorello LaGuardia and the Making of Modern New York*. New York: Penguin Group, 1989.

Kisselhoff, Jeff. *You Must Remember This: An Oral History of Manhattan from the 1890s to World War II*. New York: Harcourt Brace Jovanovich, 1989.

Kleeman, Werner. *From Dachau to D-Day*. New York: Marble House Editions, 2006.

Leeds, Mark. *Ethnic New York: A Complete Guide to the Many Faces & Cultures of New York*. Chicago: Passport Books, a division of NTC Publishing Group, 1991.

Lindbergh, Charles A. *The Wartime Journals*. New York: Harcourt Brace Jovanovich, 1970.

Lingeman, Richard. *Don't You Know There's a War On? The American Home Front, 1940–1945*. New York: G.P. Putman's Sons, 1970.

Lowenstein, Steven M. *Frankfurt on the Hudson: The German-Jewish Community of Washington Heights, 1933–1983, Its Structure and Culture*. Detroit: Wayne State University Press, 1989.

Maeder, Jay, series editor. *Big Town/Big Time, A New York Epic: 1898–1998*. New York: Daily News Books, 1999.

Mann, Klaus. *The Turning Point*. New York: L.B. Fischer, 1942.

Mead, William B. *Baseball Goes to War*. Washington, D.C.: Farragut Publishing Co., 1985.

Miller, Marvin D. *Wunderlich's Salute*. New York: Malamud-Rose Publishers, 1983.

Molnár, Ferenc. *Companion in Exile: Notes for an Autobiography*. New York: Gaer Associates, 1950.

Morison, Samuel Eliot. *History of the United States Naval Operations in World War II: The Battle of the Atlantic, Volume One*. Boston: Little, Brown and Company, 1947.

Norris, Robert S. *Racing for the Bomb: General Leslie R. Groves, The Manhattan Project's Indispensable Man*. South Royalton, Vermont: Steerforth Press, 2002.

O'Connor, Richard. *The German-Americans: An Informal History*. Boston: Little, Brown and Company, 1968.

Okrent, Daniel. *Great Fortune: The Epic of Rockefeller Center*. New York: Penguin Group, 2003.

Pfanner, Helmut F. *Exile in New York: German and Austrian Writers after 1933*. Detroit: Wayne State University Press, 1983.

Phillips, Cabell. *The 1940s: Decade of Triumph and Trouble*. New York: Macmillan Publishing Co., 1975.

Pinza, Ezio, with Robert Magidoff. *Ezio Pinza: An Autobiography.* New York: Alfred A. Knopf, Inc., 1958.

Rachlis, Eugene. *They Came to Kill: The Story of Eight Nazi Saboteurs in America.* New York: Random House, 1961.

Rollins, Richard. *I Find Treason: The Story of an American Anti-Nazi Agent.* New York: William Morrow and Company, 1941.

Roussel, Christine. *The Guide to the Art of Rockefeller Center.* New York: W. W. Norton & Company, 2006.

Sanders, Ronald. *The Days Grow Short: The Life and Music of Kurt Weill.* New York: Holt, Rinehart & Winston, 1980.

Starr, Tama, and Edward Hayman. *Signs and Wonders: The Spectacular Marketing of America.* New York: Currency (a division of Bantam Doubleday Dell Publishing Group), 1998.

Stern, Fritz. *Five Germanys I Have Known.* New York: Farrar, Straus and Giroux, 2006.

Sypher, F. J. *The Yorkville Civic Council: A Retrospective.* New York: The Yorkville Civic Council, 1991.

Tauranac, John. *The Empire State Building: The Making of a Landmark.* New York: Scribner, 1995.

Taylor, Theodore. *Fire on the Beaches.* New York: W.W. Norton & Company, 1958.

Tell, Darcy. *Times Square Spectacular: Lighting Up Broadway.* New York: Smithsonian Books (a division of HarperCollins Publishers), 2007.

Traub, James. *The Devil's Playground: A Century of Pleasure and Profit in Times Square.* New York: Random House, 2004.

Van Meter, Jonathan. *The Last Good Time.* New York: Crown Publishers, 2003.

Walters, Barbara. *Audition: A Memoir.* New York: Alfred A. Knopf, 2008.

Ward, Geoffrey C., and Ken Burns. *The War: An Intimate History 1941–1945.* New York: Alfred A. Knopf, 2007.

Willensky, Elliot. *When Brooklyn Was the World: 1920–1957.* New York: Harmony Books, 1986.

Wilson, Sondra Kathryn. *Meet Me at the Theresa: The Story of Harlem's Most Famous Hotel.* New York: Atria Books, 2004.

Yellin, Emily. *Our Mothers' War: American Women at Home and at the Front During World War II.* New York: The Free Press, 2004.

Periodicals

The New Yorker, Talk of the Town, Dec. 13, 1941.

The New Yorker, Talk of the Town, Dec. 27, 1941.

Seaport: New York's History Magazine, vol. 26, no. 2 (Summer 1992).

Rosenberg, Elliot. "Fiorello's Army," *Seaport: New York's History Magazine,* vol. 29, no. 2 (Summer 1995).

Photography Credits

★ ★

Feininger/The Collection/Time & Life Inc./ Getty Images: 114.

Frank Bauman/The LOOK Collection/Museum of the City of New York: 208.

Franklin D. Roosevelt Library: 137, 162, 163, 176.

Kurt Hulton/Hulton Archive/Getty Images: 29, 38.

Hy Deskin/Museum of the City of New York: 194.

The La Guardia and Wagner Archives, La Guardia Community College/The City University of New York: 44, 45, 132, 139, 224, 243, 247.

Library of Congress: 9, 58, 63, 70 (upper image), 73, 77, 79, 88–89, 106, 107, 116, 124, 134, 144 (lower image), 150, 152–153, 160, 182, 213, 228, 229, 231 (lower image), 233.

Meyers Rohowsky/Museum of the City of New York: 69.

The Museum of Modern Art © /Licensed by SCALA Art Resources, NY: 188.

National Museum of American Jewish History, courtesy of the USHMM Photo Archives: 2.

Naval History and Heritage Command: 103.

New York Transit Museum: 122, 206.

N.Y. Daily News: 21, 76, 119, 126, 231 (upper image).

Photofest: 140, 184, 187, 190, 204.

R. W. Shipman/Print Archive/Museum of the City of New York: 120.

Rockefeller Group Inc. © 2009/Rockefeller Center Archives: 68, 84, 92, 144 (upper image), 145, 151, 158, 168.

Sueddeutsche Zeitung Photo: 16, 18.

Sol Libsohn/The LOOK Collection/Museum of the City of New York: 170.

U.S. Army Chemical Corps Museum, Fort Leonard Wood, Missouri: 82.

U.S. Coast Guard Historian's Office: 100.

U.S. Holocaust Memorial Museum Photo Archives: 12, 17, 34.

Index

★ ★

Page numbers in *italics* refer to illustrations.

GAYLORD